Family Reunion

BOOKS BY OGDEN NASH

OGDEN NASH

Family Reunion

Boston
LITTLE, BROWN AND COMPANY
1950

Published November 1950
Reprinted November 1950

811.

Published simultaneously
in Canada by McClelland and Stewart Limited

PRINTED IN THE UNITED STATES OF AMERICA

FOREWORD

I am suddenly conscious of the fact that in a few months it will be twenty years since the publication of my first book of verse. Sobered by the impending anniversary, I set myself to reread *Hard Lines* and the nine books that followed it, an experience as unnerving as hearing a record of your own voice for the first time. In the impersonal light of retrospect, old unnoticed misdemeanors grow into whopping felonies, and you wonder how it is possible to have sinned in so many and such conflicting ways. Here is a piece of outrageous sentimentality, and next to it one of shoddy cynicism; vulgarisms march side by side with affectation; the shadows of haste and laziness fall across too many pages. And I must admit that the exuberance of youth, particularly your own, is constantly irritating to the hard-won resignation of middle age. Of course, fairness reminds me that I must be more tolerant of my twenty-eight- and thirty-eight-year-old selves than they would be of me; still, I should dearly love a chance to rewrite their stuff.

This chance, in a way, has been offered me. Mr. Angus Cameron of Little, Brown and Company, probably startled one day to realize that some fifteen hundred of my verses are in print around his office, asked me if there was among them enough suitable material to make a book for children. The answer was that I would rather make him a book for the family, which is a unit composed not only of children,

[v]

but of men, women, an occasional animal, and the common cold.

I have been a member of one family or another all my life. I think families are interesting. Only in the family do we find the battle between the sexes raging concurrently with the battle between the generations. It fascinates me to note the various ways in which a husband can please or infuriate a wife and a wife can baffle or butter up a husband; I follow with delight the vacillations of both between pride and despair when facing their young; and I can sympathize with if not approve the attempts of the young to muscle in on such adult monopolies as interrupting, talking back, staying up late, and evading the issue.

The result of this preoccupation with family relationships has been many verses scattered through several books over many years. I have here selected a group of those which, to my mind at least, seem still to stand up fairly firmly, by which I mean that the writer can read them without visibly wincing. Since I have taken full advantage of this chance to cut, whittle, and generally revise, the faults that remain must be ascribed to my current, not my youthful self.

I hope that here and there in the collection a husband and wife may come across a line that will remind them of each other, and of what it is like to shepherd a child from diapers to driver's license; and that any reasonably bright infant may gain an insight into a parent's mind that will enable him to adjust his tantrums to best effect.

CONTENTS

[vii]

[viii]

Part II

DADDY, I WANT A PET FOR MY VERY OWN, I PROMISE TO TAKE CARE OF IT

Part III

AROUND THE HOUSE, OR, WHAT PARENTS THINK ABOUT WHEN THEY AREN'T THINKING ABOUT CHILDREN

[xi]

PART ONE

THE MAN IS FATHER OF THE CHILD,
OR,
BUT HE NEVER QUITE GETS USED TO IT

THE BOY WHO LAUGHED AT SANTA CLAUS

In Baltimore there lived a boy.
He wasn't anybody's joy.
Although his name was Jabez Dawes,
His character was full of flaws.
In school he never led his classes,
He hid old ladies' reading glasses,
His mouth was open when he chewed,
And elbows to the table glued.

He stole the milk of hungry kittens,
And walked through doors marked No ADMITTANCE.
He said he acted thus because
There wasn't any Santa Claus.
Another trick that tickled Jabez
Was crying "Boo!" at little babies.
He brushed his teeth, they said in town,
Sideways instead of up and down.

Yet people pardoned every sin,
And viewed his antics with a grin,
Till they were told by Jabez Dawes,
"There isn't any Santa Claus!"
Deploring how he did behave,
His parents swiftly sought their grave.
They hurried through the portals pearly,
And Jabez left the funeral early.

Like whooping cough, from child to child,
He sped to spread the rumor wild:
"Sure as my name is Jabez Dawes
There isn't any Santa Claus!"

[3]

Slunk like a weasel or a marten
Through nursery and kindergarten,
Whispering low to every tot,
"There isn't any, no there's not!"

The children wept all Christmas Eve
And Jabez chortled up his sleeve.
No infant dared hang up his stocking
For fear of Jabez' ribald mocking.
He sprawled on his untidy bed,
Fresh malice dancing in his head,
When presently with scalp a-tingling,
Jabez heard a distant jingling;
He heard the crunch of sleigh and hoof
Crisply alighting on the roof.

What good to rise and bar the door?
A shower of soot was on the floor.
What was beheld by Jabez Dawes?
The fireplace full of Santa Claus!
Then Jabez fell upon his knees
With cries of "Don't," and "Pretty please."
He howled, "I don't know where you read it,
But anyhow, I never said it!"

"Jabez," replied the angry saint,
"It isn't I, it's you that ain't.
Although there is a Santa Claus,
There isn't any Jabez Dawes!"
Said Jabez then with impudent vim,
"Oh, yes there is; and I am him!

Your magic don't scare me, it doesn't" —
And suddenly he found he wasn't!

From grimy feet to grimy locks,
Jabez became a Jack-in-the-box,
An ugly toy with springs unsprung,
Forever sticking out his tongue.
The neighbors heard his mournful squeal;
They searched for him, but not with zeal.
No trace was found of Jabez Dawes,
Which led to thunderous applause,
And people drank a loving cup
And went and hung their stockings up.

All you who sneer at Santa Claus,
Beware the fate of Jabez Dawes,
The saucy boy who mocked the saint.
Donder and Blitzen licked off his paint.

DID SOMEONE SAY "BABIES"?

Everybody who has a baby thinks everybody who hasn't
    a baby ought to have a baby,
Which accounts for the success of such plays as the Irish
    Rose of Abie,
The idea apparently being that just by being fruitful
You are doing something beautiful,
Which if it is true
Means that the common housefly is several million times
    more beautiful than me or you.
Who is responsible for this propaganda that fills all our
    houses from their attics to their kitchens?

Is it the perambulator trust or the safety pin manufacturers or the census takers or the obstetritchens?

Men and women everywhere would have a lot more chance of acquiring recreation and fame and financial independence

If they didn't have to spend most of their time and money tending and supporting two or three unattractive descendants.

We could soon upset this kettle of fish, forsooth,

If every adult would only come out and tell every other adult the truth.

To arms, adults! Kindle the beacon fires!

Women, do you want to be nothing but dams? Men, do you want to be nothing but sires?

To arms, Mr. President! Call out the army, the navy, the marines, the militia, the cadets and the middies.

Down with the kiddies!

TO A SMALL BOY STANDING ON MY SHOES
WHILE I AM WEARING THEM

Let's straighten this out, my little man,
And reach an agreement if we can.
I entered your door as an honored guest.
My shoes are shined and my trousers are pressed,
And I won't stretch out and read you the funnies
And I won't pretend that we're Easter bunnies.
If you must get somebody down on the floor,
What do you think your parents are for?
I do not like the things that you say
And I hate the games that you want to play.

No matter how frightfully hard you try,
We've little in common, you and I.
The interest I take in my neighbor's nursery
Would have to grow, to be even cursory,
And I would that performing sons and nephews
Were carted away with the daily refuse,
And I hold that frolicsome daughters and nieces
Are ample excuse for breaking leases.
You may take a sock at your daddy's tummy,
Or climb all over your doting mummy,
But keep your attentions to me in check,
Or, sonny boy, I will wring your neck.
A happier man today I'd be
Had someone wrung it ahead of me.

PEDIATRIC REFLECTION

Many an infant that screams like a calliope
Could be soothed by a little attention to its diope.

SOME OF MY BEST FRIENDS ARE CHILDREN

Ichneumons are fond of little ichneumons,
And lions of little lions,
But I am not fond of little humans;
I do not believe in scions.

Of course there's always our child,
But our child is different,
Our child appeals

[7]

To the cultivated mind.
Ours is a lady;
Boys are odoriferant;
Ladies are the sweetness;
Boys are the rind.

Whenever whimsy collides with whimsy
As parents compare their cherubs,
At the slightest excuse, however flimsy,
I fold my tent like the Arubs.

Of course there's always our child,
But our child is charminger,
Our child's eyes
Are a special kind of blue;
Our child's smile
Is quite a lot disarminger;
Our child's tooth
Is very nearly through.

Mankind, I consider, attained its zenith
The day it achieved the adult;
When the conversation to infants leaneth,
My horse is bridled and saddult.

Of course there's always our child,
But our child is wittier;
Our child's noises
Are the nicest kind of noise;
She has no beard
Like Tennyson or Whittier;
But Tennyson and Whittier
Began as little boys.

The Politician, the Parent, the Preacher,
Were each of them once a kiddie.
The child is indeed a talented creature.
Do I want one? Heaven forbidde!

Of course there's always our child
But our child's adorable.
Our child's an angel
Fairer than the flowers;
Our child fascinates
One who's rather borable;
And incidentally,
Our child is ours.

REFLECTION ON BABIES

A bit of talcum
Is always walcum.

AFTER THE CHRISTENING

Come along, everybody, see the pretty baby,
Such a pretty baby ought to be adored.
Come along, everybody, come and bore the baby,
See the pretty baby, begging to be bored.

Hurry, hurry, Aunt Louise,
Silly names are sure to please.
Bother what the baby thinks!
Call her Kitchy-kitch and Binks,

Call her Wackywoo and Snookums,
Just ignore her dirty lookums,
Who than she is fairer game
For every kind of silly name?
Baby cannot answer back,
Or perhaps an aunt she'd lack.

Come along, everybody, isn't she a darling?
Such a little darling ought to be enjoyed.
Come along, everybody, let's annoy the baby,
Such a darling darling begs to be annoyed.

Goodness Gracious, Uncle George!
Home at last from Valley Forge?
Won't you try on her the whoops
That cheered the Continental troops?
Stand a little closer, please;
That will put her at her ease;
And babies find it hard to hear,
So place your mouth against her ear —
I guess she heard it, Uncle George;
I'm sure they did at Valley Forge.

Come along, everybody, see the little lady,
Isn't she adorable and kissable and pleasing?
Come along, everybody, come and tease the baby,
Here's a lady baby available for teasing!

Cousin Charles was always chummy;
He's about to poke her tummy.
Grandpa almost chokes on chuckles,
Tickling with his beard her knuckles;

All of Granny's muscles ache
From half an hour of patty-cake;
God-mamma with glee begins
A noisy count of baby's chins;
God-papa with humor glows
Playing piggie with her toes.
See the happy prideful parents,
Do they think of interference?
Certainly not, while baby gives
Such wholesome fun to relatives.

Up and at her, everybody, at the pretty baby,
Tell her she's a dumpling, tell her she's a dear.
Everybody knows the way to woo a baby —
Tickle her and pinch her and yodel in her ear.

IT MUST BE THE MILK

There is a thought that I have tried not to but cannot help
    but think,
Which is, My goodness how much infants resemble people
    who have had too much to drink.
Tots and sots, so different and yet so identical!
What a humiliating coincidence for pride parental!
Yet when you see your little dumpling set sail across the
    nursery floor,
Can you conscientiously deny the resemblance to some-
    body who is leaving a tavern after having tried to
    leave it a dozen times and each time turned back for
    just one more?
Each step achieved

Is simply too good to be believed;
Foot somehow follows foot
And somehow manages to stay put;
Arms wildly semaphore,
Wild eyes seem to ask, Whatever did we get in such a
dilemma for?
And their gait is more that of a duckling than a Greek
goddessling or godling,
And in inebriates it's called staggering but in infants it's
called toddling.
Another kinship with topers is also by infants exhibited,
Which is that they are completely uninhibited,
And they can't talk straight
Any more than they can walk straight;
Their pronunciation is awful
And their grammar is flawful,
And in adults it's drunken and maudlin and deplorable,
But in infants it's tunnin' and adorable.
So I hope you will agree that it is very hard to tell an in-
fant from somebody who has gazed too long into
the cup,
And really the only way you can tell them apart is to
wait till next day, and the infant is the one that feels
all right when it wakes up.

IN WHICH THE POET IS ASHAMED
BUT PLEASED

Of all the things that I would rather,
It is to be my daughter's father,
While she, with innocence divine,
Is quite contented to be mine.

I am distressingly aware
That this arrangement is unfair,
For I, when in my celibate garrison,
Acquired some standard of comparison.

I visited nurseries galore,
Compiled statistics by the score,
And gained experience from a crew
Of children passing in review.

I saw the best that parents vaunted;
They weren't exactly what I wanted;
Yet, all the offspring that I faced,
They served to cultivate my taste.

Thus, let the miser praise the mintage,
And let the vintner praise the vintage;
I'm conscious that in praising her,
I'm speaking as a connoisseur.

While she, poor dear, has never known
A father other than her own.
She wots of other girls' papas
No more than of the Persian Shah's.

Within her head no notion stirs
That some are better men than hers;
That some are richer, some are kinder,
Some are solider, some refineder,

That some are vastly more amusing
Some fitter subjects for enthusing,

That some are cleverer, some are braver,
Than the one that fortune gave her.

What fortune set us side by side,
Her scope so narrow, mine so wide?
We owe to this sweet dispensation
Our mutual appreciation.

OUR CHILD DOESN'T KNOW ANYTHING

OR

THANK HEAVEN!

I am now about to make a remark that I suppose most
    parents will think me hateful for,
Though as a matter of fact I am only commenting on a
    condition that they should be more than grateful for.
What I want to say is, that of luckiness it seems to me to
    be the height
That babies aren't very bright.
Now listen to me for a minute, all you proud progenitors
    who boast that your bedridden infant offspring of two
    months or so are already bright enough to get into
    Harvard or Stanford or Notre Dame or Fordham;
Don't you realize that the only thing that makes life at all
    bearable to those selfsame offspring is being rather
    backward, and that if they had any sense at all they
    would lose no time in perishing of boredom?
Good heavens, I can think of no catastrophe more immense
Than a baby with sense,
Because one thing at least, willy-nilly, you must believe,
And that is, that a baby has twenty-four hours a day to
    get through with just the same as we've.

Some people choose to wonder about virtue and others about crime,
But I choose to wonder how babies manage to pass the time.
They can't pass it in tennis or badminton or golf,
Or in going around rescuing people from Indians and then marrying somebody else the way Pocahontas did with Messrs. Smith and Rolfe;
They can't pass it in bridge or parchesi or backgammon,
Or in taking the subway to Wall Street and worshiping of Mammon;
How then do they manage to enthuse themselves,
And amuse themselves?
Well, partly they sleep,
And mostly they weep,
And the rest of the time they relax
On their backs,
And eat, by régime specifically, but by nature omnivorously,
And vocalize vocivorously.
That, to make it short,
Is about all they can do in the way of sport;
So whatever may come,
I am glad that babies are dumb.
I shudder to think what for entertainment they would do
Were they as bright as me or you.

SONG TO BE SUNG BY THE FATHER OF INFANT FEMALE CHILDREN

My heart leaps up when I behold
A rainbow in the sky;
Contrariwise, my blood runs cold

When little boys go by.
For little boys as little boys,
No special hate I carry,
But now and then they grow to men,
And when they do, they marry.
No matter how they tarry,
Eventually they marry.
And, swine among the pearls,
They marry little girls.

Oh, somewhere, somewhere, an infant plays,
With parents who feed and clothe him.
Their lips are sticky with pride and praise,
But I have begun to loathe him.
Yes, I loathe with a loathing shameless
This child who to me is nameless.
This bachelor child in his carriage
Gives never a thought to marriage,
But a person can hardly say knife
Before he will hunt him a wife.

I never see an infant (male),
A-sleeping in the sun,
Without I turn a trifle pale
And think Is *he* the one?
Oh, first he'll want to crop his curls,
And then he'll want a pony,
And then he'll think of pretty girls
And holy matrimony.
He'll put away his pony,
And sigh for matrimony.
A cat without a mouse
Is he without a spouse.

Oh, somewhere he bubbles bubbles of milk,
And quietly sucks his thumbs.
His cheeks are roses painted on silk,
And his teeth are tucked in his gums.
But alas, the teeth will begin to grow,
And the bubbles will cease to bubble;
Given a score of years or so,
The roses will turn to stubble.
He'll sell a bond, or he'll write a book,
And his eyes will get that acquisitive look,
And raging and ravenous for the kill,
He'll boldly ask for the hand of Jill.
This infant whose middle
Is diapered still
Will want to marry
My daughter Jill.

Oh sweet be his slumber and moist his middle!
My dreams, I fear, are infanticiddle.
A fig for embryo Lohengrins!
I'll open all of his safety pins,
I'll pepper his powder, and salt his bottle,
And give him readings from Aristotle.
Sand for his spinach I'll gladly bring,
And Tabasco sauce for his teething ring,
And an elegant, gluttonous alligator
To play with in his perambulator.
Then perhaps he'll struggle through fire and water
To marry somebody else's daughter.

LINES TO BE EMBROIDERED ON A BIB

OR

THE CHILD IS FATHER OF THE MAN, BUT NOT FOR QUITE A WHILE

So Thomas Edison
Never drank his medicine;
So Blackstone and Hoyle
Refused cod-liver oil;
So Sir Thomas Malory
Never heard of a calory;
So the Earl of Lennox
Murdered Rizzio without the aid of vitamins or calisthenox;
So Socrates and Plato
Ate dessert without finishing their potato;
So spinach was too spinachy
For Leonardo da Vinaci;
Well, it's all immaterial,
So eat your nice cereal,
And if you want to name your own ration,
First go get a reputation.

THE RETURN

Early is the evening,
Reluctant the dawn;
Once there was a summer;
Sudden it was gone.
It fell like a leaf;
Whirled downstream.
Was there ever summer,

[18]

Or only a dream?
Was ever a world
That was not November?
Once there was summer,
And this I remember,

Cornflowers and daisies,
Buttercups and clover,
Black-eyed Susans, and Queen Anne's lace;
A wide green meadow,
And the bees booming over,
And a little laughing girl with the wind in her face.

Strident are the voices
And hard lights shine;
Feral are the faces;
Is one of them mine?
Something is lost now;
Tarnished the gleam;
Was there ever nobleness,
Or only a dream?
Yes, and it lingers,
Lost not yet;
Something remains
Till this I forget,

Cornflowers and clover,
Buttercups and daisies,
Black-eyed Susans under blue and white skies;
And the grass waist-high
Where the red cow grazes,
And a little laughing girl with faith in her eyes.

"MY CHILD IS PHLEGMATIC . . ."

— Anxious Parent

Anxious Parent, I guess you have just never been around;

I guess you just don't know who are the happiest people
anywhere to be found;

So you are worried, are you, because your child is turning out to be phlegmatic?

Forgive me if I seem a trifle unsympathatic.

Why do you want your child to be a flashing, coruscating
gem?

Don't you know the only peace the world can give lies
not in flame but in phlegm?

Don't you know that the people with souls of putty

Are the only people who are sitting prutty?

They never get all worked up at the drop of a pin or a
feather or a hat,

They never go around saying bitterly to themselves: "Oh
Lord, did I really do, did I really say that?"

They never bother their heads about injustice,

It doesn't disturb them that stupidity always gets there with
the mostest fustes'.

No, when they eat they digest their food, and when they
go to bed they get right to sleep,

And four phlegmatic angels a stolid watch over them keep.

Oh to be phlegmatic, oh to be stolid, oh to be torpid,
oh to be calm!

For it is only thus, Anxious Parent, that we can get through
life without a qualm.

RAINY DAY

Linell is clad in a gown of green,
She walks in state like a fairy queen.
Her train is tucked in a winsome bunch
Directly behind her royal lunch.
With a dignified skip and a haughty hop
Her golden slippers go clippety-clop.
I think I am Ozma, says Linell.
I'm Ozma too, says Isabel.

Linell has discovered a filmy veil;
The very thing for a swishy tail.
The waves wash over the nursery floor
And break on the rug with a rumbling roar;
The swishy tail gives a swishy swish;
She's off and away like a frightened fish.
Now I'm a mermaid, says Linell.
I'm mermaid too, says Isabel.

Her trousers are blue, her hair is kinky,
Her jacket is red and her skin is inky.
She is hiding behind a green umbrella;
She couldn't be Alice, or Cinderella,
Or Puss in Boots, or the Fiddlers Three;
Goodness gracious, who *can* she be?
I'm Little Black Sambo, says Linell.
I'm Sambo, too, says Isabel.

Clack the shutters. The blinds are drawn.
Click the switch, and the lights are gone.
Linell is under the blankets deep,

Murmuring down the hill to sleep.
Oh, deep in the soft and gentle dark
She stirs and chirps like a drowsy lark.
I love you, Mummy, says Linell.
Love Mummy too, says Isabel.

DON'T CRY, DARLING, IT'S BLOOD
ALL RIGHT

Whenever poets want to give you the idea that something
    is particularly meek and mild,
They compare it to a child,
Thereby proving that though poets with poetry may be
    rife
They don't know the facts of life.
If of compassion you desire either a tittle or a jot,
Don't try to get it from a tot.
Hard-boiled, sophisticated adults like me and you
May enjoy ourselves thoroughly with *Little Women* and
    Winnie-the-Pooh,
But innocent infants these titles from their reading course
    eliminate
As soon as they discover that it was honey and nuts and
    mashed potatoes instead of human flesh that Winnie-
    the-Pooh and Little Women ate.
Innocent infants have no use for fables about rabbits or
    donkeys or tortoises or porpoises,
What they want is something with plenty of well-mutilated
    corpoises.
Not on legends of how the rose came to be a rose instead
    of a petunia is their fancy fed,

But on the inside story of how somebody's bones got
    ground up to make somebody else's bread.
They'll go to sleep listening to the story of the little beggar-
    maid who got to be queen by being kind to the bees
    and the birds,
But they're all eyes and ears the minute they suspect a
    wolf or a giant is going to tear some poor woodcutter
    into quarters or thirds.
It really doesn't take much to fill their cup;
All they want is for somebody to be eaten up.
Therefore I say unto you, all you poets who are so crazy
    about meek and mild little children and their angelic
    air,
If you are sincere and really want to please them, why
    just go out and get yourselves devoured by a bear.

ONE, TWO, BUCKLE MY SHOE

Roses red and jonquils gold,
I know a girl who is two years old.
Hyacinth white and violets blue,
She was very good, so now she's two.
The rabbit there on the corner shelf,
He wishes that he were two, himself,
And Little Bo Peep on the silver cup
Says, "Gracious, Linell is growing up!"
And the faithful music box simply burns
To wish her many happy returns.
The cows in the meadow murmur, "Moo!
To think that child has arrived at two!"
The cows in the meadow moo and mutter,

And send their specialest milk and butter.
The cardinal on the window sill
Greets the news with an extra trill,
The mocking bird and the dandy jay
With kindest respect salute the day,
And the swaggering crow admits his awe,
Cawing a splendid birthday caw,
And the squirrel hoists his bushy tail
In the squirrel manner of crying "Hail!"

Roses red and violets blue,
I know a girl who is really two.
Yesterday she was only one;
Today, I think, will be twice the fun.
For all good things come double fold
When a good girl gets to be two years old.
Double the number of stairs to climb,
And maybe some of them two at a time;
Double the songs and double the dances,
Double the grave and merry fancies;
Double the dolls to undress and scrub,
Double the ducks in the evening tub;
Double walks in exciting lanes,
And double trips to wave at the trains;
And certainly, double stories told
When a good girl gets to be two years old.
Linell, Linell, is it really true?
Do you faithfully promise that you are two?
Kiss me again for a lucky start,
And Happy Birthday, with twice my heart.

JUDGMENT DAY

This is the day, this is the day!
I knew as soon as the sun's first ray
Crept through the slats of the cot,
And opened the eyes of a tot,
And the tot would rather have slept,
And, therefore, wept.
This is the day that is wrong,
The day when the only song
Is a skirling lamentation
Of continuous indignation,
When the visage is ireful,
The voice, direful,
And the early, pearly teeth
Snick like a sword in the sheath,
When the fists are clenched,
And the cheeks are drenched
In full-fed freshets and tumbling, tumultuous torrents
Of virtuous abhorrence,
When loud as the challenging trumpets of John at Lepanto
Rings the clarion, "I don't want to."
This is the day, the season,
Of wrongs without reason,
The day when the prunes and the cereal
Taste like building material,
When the spinach tastes only like spinach, and honey and
        sugar
Raise howls like the yowls of a quarrelsome puma or cougar,
When the wail is not to be hushed
Nor the hair to be brushed,
When life is frustration, and either

A person must be all alone or have somebody with her,
    and tolerates neither,
When outdoors is worse than in, and indoors than out,
    and both too dull to be borne,
And dolls are flung under the bed and books are torn,
When people humiliate a person
With their clumsily tactful attempts to conciliate a person,
When music no charm possesses,
Nor hats, nor mittens, nor dresses,
When the frowning fortress is woe
And the watchword is No.
You owners of children who pass this day with forbear-
    ance,
You indeed are parents!

THUNDER OVER THE NURSERY

Listen to me, angel tot,
Whom I love an awful lot,
It will save a barrel of bother
If we understand each other.

Every time that I'm your herder
You think you get away with murder.
All right, infant, so you do,
But only because I want you to.

Baby's muscles are prodigious,
Baby's beautiful, not higious,
She can talk and walk and run
Like a daughter of a gun.

Well, you may be a genius, child,
And I a parent dull and mild;
In spite of which, and nevertheless,
I could lick you yet, I guess.

Forgive me, pet, if I am frank,
But truth is money in the bank;
I wish you to admire and love yourself,
But not to get too far above yourself.

When we race, you always win;
Baby, think before you grin.
It may occur to you, perhaps,
That Daddy's running under wraps.

When you hide behind the chair
And Daddy seeks you everywhere,
Behind the door, beneath the bed —
That's Daddy's heart, not Baby's head.

When I praise your speech in glee
And claim you talk as well as me,
That's the spirit, not the letter.
I know more words, and say them better.

In future, then, when I'm your herder,
Continue getting away with murder;
But know from him who murder endures,
It's his idea much more than yours.

Once there was a poem, and it wasn't by Edgar A. Guest,
And it said children ought to agree like little birdies in
    their nest.
Oh forsooth forsooth!
That poem was certainly more poetry than truth,
Because do you believe that little birdies in their nest
    agree?
It doesn't sound very probable to me.
Ah no, but I can tell you what does sound probable,
And that is that life in a nest is just one long quarrel and
    squabbable.
Look at that young mother robin over in that elm, or is
    it a beech,
She has two little robins and she thinks she has solved
    her problem because she has learned not to bring
    home just one worm but a worm for each.
She is very pleased with her understanding of fledgling
    psychology, but in just about two minutes she is go-
    ing to lose a year's growth,
Because she's going to find that one little robin gets no
    worms and the other little robin gets both,
And if one little robin gets out of the nest on the wrong
    side and nothing can please it,
Why the other little robin will choose that moment to tease
    it,
And if one little robin starts a game the other little robin
    will stop it,
And if one little robin builds a castle the other little
    robin will knock it down and if one little robin blows
    a bubble the other little robin will pop it.

[28   ]

Yes, I bet that if you walked up to any nest and got a good revealing glimpse,

Why, you would find that our little feathered friendlets disagree just like human imps,

And I also bet that their distracted feathered parents quote feathered poetry to them by whoever the most popular feathered poet may be,

All about why don't they like little children in their nurseries agree.

Well, to put the truth about youth in a very few words,

Why the truth is that little birds do agree like children and children do agree like little birds,

Because you take offspring, and I don't care whether a house or a tree is their abode,

They may love each other but they aren't going to agree with each other anywhere except in an ode.

It doesn't seem to have occurred to the poet,

That nobody agrees with anybody else anyhow, but adults conceal it and infants show it.

ODE TO C. B. E., PRACTICALLY THE ONLY NEW MALE CHILD I KNOW OF

Hail, third-born infant of my friend,
Thou rosy extra dividend!
What mirth enlivens thy vicinity,
Thou handsome example of masculinity!
Thou rugged atom, thou hairless he-man,
Potential President or G-man!
Thy parents said they didn't care
Were thou an heiress or an heir.

[29]

"It's all the same to us," they cried.
Good gracious, how thy parents lied!
Thy father bounded like a squirrel
When scientists pronounced thee virile;
Thy mother danced upon her cot
When told a daughter thou wert not;
Thy sisters' eyes with glee did glister
At doing without another sister;
And o'er Manhattan, from river to river,
There ran a thrill, there ran a quiver.
The buildings rocked, the bridges trembled,
As males in milling hordes assembled;
A million men, agog and eager,
The lucky hospital did beleaguer
To pop their eyes and crane their necks
At the new addition to their sex,
As well they might, to calm their fears;
Thou wert the first in years and years,
And fathers gazed in wild despair
At daughters, daughters everywhere.
Oh, late and early, night and morn,
Nothing but girls was being born;
Then, as the scornfulest of affronts,
They started coming five at once.
And men were filled with thickening gloom
At prospects of their sex's doom;
The future fraught with meek surrender
To the overwhelming feminine gender;
A world of regnant Amazons,
Perkinses, Roosevelts, and Dionnes.
But now they glimpse in thine arrival
A fighting chance for man's survival.

All hail the man who had a son!
Others can do what he has done!
And hail to thee, thou hopeful token
Of feminine fetters finally broken!
Yea, thanks to thee, this spinning ball
May be a man's world after all.

BABY, WHAT MAKES THE SKY BLUE?

Oh, what a tangled web do parents weave
When they think that their children are naïve,
Because the moment they look on their little ones as country
cousins and themselves as suave and sophisticated,
Why, that is the moment they are not only going to get
their feelings hurt but also end up totally baffled and
mysticated,
Because you take sophisticated you, and you know that
your radio is more magical than anything out of Ander-
sen or the Brothers Grimm,
But you take ingenuous Junior, and it's just a radio to him,
And you carefully explain all about Marconi and sound
waves and static and where the broadcast comes from
and how it gets here to the tot,
And he simply says Why not?
Yes, one very good reason children should be seen and not
heard
Is that to ingenuous them, a telephone or a television or an
electric refrigerator is no more awe-inspiring than a
flower or a bird,
Because they live in a world that every day produces something that if they didn't cultivate a calm acceptance of
the impossible would strain their belief,

So their approach to gadgets is that if they can accept the
sun and moon why they guess they can accept the
Yankee Clipper and the Super-Chief.
Sophisticated parents live agog in a world that to them is
enchanted;
Ingenuous children just naïvely take it for granted.

THE FACTS OF LIFE

Daughter, dim those reverent eyes;
Daddy must apologize.
Daddy's not an engineer;
Never will be, now, I fear.
Daddy couldn't drive a train,
Not for all the sherry in Spain.

Daddy's not a fireman, too;
He couldn't do what firemen do.
Clanging bells and screaming sirens
Are no part of his environs.
In case of fire, no hero he;
Merely a humble rescuee.

Also, greatly to his grief,
Daddy's not an Indian chief.
Daddy cannot stealthy walk
Or wield a lethal tomahawk.
Hark to Daddy's secret grim:
Feathers only tickle him.

Better learn it now than later:
Daddy's not an aviator.

Daddy cannot soar and swoop,
Neither can he loop the loop.
Parachutes he never hung on to,
And what is worse, he doesn't want to.

As long as Daddy's being defiant,
Daddy, child, is not a giant.
You'll travel far if you would seek
A less remarkable physique.
That's why he feels a decade older
When you are riding on his shoulder.

Another thing that Daddy ain't,
I frankly tell you, is a saint.
Daddy, my faithful catechumen,
Is widely known as all too human.
Still, if you watch him, you will find
He does his best, when so inclined.

One final skeleton while I dare:
Daddy's not a millionaire.
Alas, his most amusing verse
Is not a Fortunatus purse.
What I should buy for you, my sweeting,
Did journals end in both ends meeting!

There, child, you have the dismal truth,
Now obvious as a missing tooth.
Your doom it is to be the daughter
Of one as romantic as soapy water.
Should you like it, you'd overwhelm me,
And if you hate it, please don't tell me.

LITTLE FEET

Oh, who would live in a silent house,
As still as a waltz left unwritten by Strauss,
As undisturbed as a virgin dewdrop,
And quiet enough to hear a shoe drop?
Who would dwell
In a vacuum cell,
In a home as mute as a clapperless bell?
Oh, a home as mute as a bell that's clapperless
Is forlorn as an Indian in Indianapolis.

Then ho! for the patter of little feet,
And the childish chatter of voices sweet,
For the ringing laughter and prancing capers
That soothe your ear as you read the papers,
For the trumpets that blow and the balls that bounce
As you struggle to balance your old accounts,
For the chubby arms that encircle your neck,
And the chubby behinds that your lap bedeck,
And sirens who save their wiliest wooing
For the critical spot in whatever you're doing.

Shakespeare's, I'm sure, was a silent house,
And that of Good King Wenceslaus,
And Napoleon's dwelling, and Alexander's,
And whoever's that wrote *The Dog of Flanders*.
Yes, Shelley and Keats
And other élites,
They missed the patter of little feets,
For he who sits and listens to pattering
Will never accomplish more than a smattering.

Then ho! for the patter of little feet!
Some find these footfalls doubly sweet,
Subjecting them to the twofold use
Of paternal pride and a good excuse.
You say, for instance, my modest chanteys
Are not so fine as Pope's or Dante's?
My deeds do not compare with those
Of Nelson, or Michelangelo's?
Well, my life is perpetual Children's Hour,
Or boy! would immortal genius flower!

A GOOD PARENT'S GARDEN OF VISION

PART I: THE DREAM

In my bachelor days, no parent I,
My spirits fell as the weeks ran by,
And, tossing on my pallet, I dolefully thought
Of Time, the tri-motored Juggernaut,
Or paused at whiles amid my gardening
To listen for the sound of my arteries hardening.
But now I eagerly listen for
Senility knocking at the door.
You ask, and properly ask, no doubt,
Whence this astonishing right-about?
Why now so Frances Hodgson Bùrnett-y? —
Not Pelmanism, but paternity.
Come dotage, envelop me in your arms;
Old age, I ween, has its special charms.
I'll camp awhile by Jordan's water
And enjoy being a nuisance to my daughter.
The loving offspring of Mr. N.
Won't trouble her head with raw young men,

Young men who cry she is lissome and flowery,
Young men who inquire about her dowery.
She'll make young men all keep their distances,
She'll listen to her father's reministances,
She'll fondly lay out his favorite slippers,
And when he wears arctics she'll zip his zippers,
She'll nogg his eggs and she'll toast his kippers,
And disparage the quips of the current quippers.
She'll light his pipe and she'll mix his drinks
And conceal from her father every thought she thinks,
And he in his way and she in hern
Will be merry as a melody by Mr. Kern.

PART II: THE NIGHTMARE

And he in his way and she in hern
Will be merry as ashes in a funeral urn.
She'll discourage his pipe and she'll hide his drinks,
And she'll tell her father every thought she thinks.
She'll make audible comments on his taste in togs,
She'll put his eggs in custards and not in noggs,
She'll object to the odor of kippering kippers,
She will laugh Ha Ha! at the current quippers,
She will leave the room when he dons his slippers,
When his buttons unbutton she will advocate zippers.
She'll see that parents keep their proper distances,
And she'll give young men a lot of reministances,
She'll look at her father like a beetle from the Bowery,
And ask why she hasn't a decent dowery,
And the only moments she'll be really merry
Will be pricing plots at the cemetery,
And I fear by the time his epitaph's read,
She'll be either a spinster or five times wed.

O pleasing daughter of Mr. N.,
His forebodings are happily beyond your ken,
And I gravely doubt that his querulous words
Retard the digestion of your whey and curds,
For children all choose their own sweet way —
Say Disobey, and they Datobey.
It's not that they're all in the pay of Belial,
It's only their way of being filial.
Some grow up hideous, others beautiful,
Some ungrateful and others dutiful;
Why try to prognosticate which yours will be?
There's nothing to do but wait and see.
Only nasty parents lose their nerve
At the prospect of getting what they deserve.
With a conscience as clear as mountain water
I await the best from my loving daughter.

SEPTEMBER MORN

Oh, what in the world could be more fun
Than to have your holiday over and done;
Than to stand in a rural railway station
With fifty weeks till your next vacation!
Ah me, what jovial words are spoken
When you find the suitcase handle is broken.
You juggle golf bags and tennis rackets,
And ludicrous bulging paper packets,
You count your paraphernalia twice
From the children themselves to their milk and ice.
A whistle announces the train is coming;

You drop the children's portable plumbing;
The train draws up with a jerk and a wiggle
From the engineer's convulsive giggle,
And every window flattens the nose
Of a passenger reveling in your woes,
And the only car with an open door
Is a hundred yards behind or before.
Heave up the bags, the ice, the milk,
Heave up your struggling youthful ilk!
Heave up, heave up, and keep on heaving;
This good old train will soon be leaving.
The grim conductor, watch in hand,
Glares angrily on your hapless band.
Oh when was order e'er restored
By disgusted cries of All aboard?
This luggage on the platform piled
May well conceal a favorite child.
Conductor, cease your cry disgusted;
Distracted parents can't be trusted,
In times of stress they have been known
To ship their offspring off alone;
Not unprotected, not at large,
But in the kind conductor's charge.
Farewell, farewell to the sand and foam,
You are getting yourself and your family home.
Oh, I think there is no such capital fun
But having your teeth out one by one.

THE TALE OF CUSTARD THE DRAGON

Belinda lived in a little white house,
With a little black kitten and a little gray mouse,
And a little yellow dog and a little red wagon,
And a realio, trulio, little pet dragon.

Now the name of the little black kitten was Ink,
And the little gray mouse, she called her Blink,
And the little yellow dog was sharp as Mustard,
But the dragon was a coward, and she called him Custard.

Custard the dragon had big sharp teeth,
And spikes on top of him and scales underneath,
Mouth like a fireplace, chimney for a nose,
And realio, trulio daggers on his toes.

Belinda was as brave as a barrel full of bears,
And Ink and Blink chased lions down the stairs,
Mustard was as brave as a tiger in a rage,
But Custard cried for a nice safe cage.

Belinda tickled him, she tickled him unmerciful,
Ink, Blink and Mustard, they rudely called him Percival,
They all sat laughing in the little red wagon
At the realio, trulio, cowardly dragon.

Belinda giggled till she shook the house,
And Blink said Weeck! which is giggling for a mouse,
Ink and Mustard rudely asked his age,
When Custard cried for a nice safe cage.

Suddenly, suddenly they heard a nasty sound,
And Mustard growled, and they all looked around.

Meowch! cried Ink, and Ooh! cried Belinda,
For there was a pirate, climbing in the winda.

Pistol in his left hand, pistol in his right,
And he held in his teeth a cutlass bright,
His beard was black, one leg was wood;
It was clear that the pirate meant no good.

Belinda paled, and she cried Help! Help!
But Mustard fled with a terrified yelp,
Ink trickled down to the bottom of the household,
And little mouse Blink strategically mouseholed.

But up jumped Custard, snorting like an engine,
Clashed his tail like irons in a dungeon,
With a clatter and a clank and a jangling squirm
He went at the pirate like a robin at a worm.

The pirate gaped at Belinda's dragon,
And gulped some grog from his pocket flagon,
He fired two bullets, but they didn't hit,
And Custard gobbled him, every bit.

Belinda embraced him, Mustard licked him,
No one mourned for his pirate victim.
Ink and Blink in glee did gyrate
Around the dragon that ate the pyrate.

Belinda still lives in her little white house,
With her little black kitten and her little gray mouse,
And her little yellow dog and her little red wagon,
And her realio, trulio, little pet dragon.

Belinda is as brave as a barrel full of bears,
And Ink and Blink chase lions down the stairs.
Mustard is as brave as a tiger in a rage,
But Custard keeps crying for a nice safe cage.

CHILDREN'S PARTY

May I join you in the doghouse, Rover?
I wish to retire till the party's over.
Since three o'clock I've done my best
To entertain each tiny guest;
My conscience now I've left behind me,
And if they want me, let them find me.
I blew their bubbles, I sailed their boats,
I kept them from each other's throats.
I told them tales of magic lands,
I took them out to wash their hands.
I sorted their rubbers and tied their laces,
I wiped their noses and dried their faces.
Of similarity there's lots
'Twixt tiny tots and Hottentots.
I've earned repose to heal the ravages
Of these angelic-looking savages.
Oh, progeny playing by itself
Is a lonely fascinating elf,
But progeny in roistering batches
Would drive Saint Francis from here to Natchez.
Shunned are the games a parent proposes;
They prefer to squirt each other with hoses,
Their playmates are their natural foemen
And they like to poke each other's abdomen.

Their joy needs another's woe to cushion it
Say a puddle, and somebody littler to push in it.
They observe with glee the ballistic results
Of ice cream with spoons for catapults,
And inform the assembly with tears and glares
That everyone's presents are better than theirs.
Oh, little women and little men,
Someday I hope to love you again,
But not till after the party's over,
So give me the key to the doghouse, Rover.

A WATCHED EXAMPLE NEVER BOILS

The weather is so very mild
That some would call it warm.
Good gracious, aren't we lucky, child?
Here comes a thunderstorm.

The sky is now indelible ink,
The branches reft asunder;
But you and I, we do not shrink;
We love the lovely thunder.

The garden is a raging sea,
The hurricane is snarling;
Oh happy you and happy me!
Isn't the lightning darling?

Fear not the thunder, little one.
It's weather, simply weather;
It's friendly giants full of fun
Clapping their hands together.

I hope of lightning our supply
Will never be exhausted;
You know it's lanterns in the sky
For angels who are losted.

We love the kindly wind and hail,
The jolly thunderbolt,
We watch in glee the fairy trail
Of ampere, watt, and volt.

Oh, than to enjoy a storm like this
There's nothing I would rather.
Don't dive beneath the blankets, Miss!
Or else leave room for Father.

THE PARENT

Children aren't happy with nothing to ignore,
And that's what parents were created for.

THE BIG TENT UNDER THE ROOF

Noises new to sea and land
Issue from the circus band.
Each musician looks like mumps
From blowing umpah umpah umps.

Lovely girls in spangled pants
Ride on gilded elephants.
Elephants are useful friends,

They have handles on both ends;
They hold each other's hindmost handles
And flee from mice and Roman candles.
Their hearts are gold, their hides are emery,
And they have a most tenacious memory.

Notice also, girls and boys,
The circus horses' avoirdupois.
Far and wide the wily scouts
Seek these snow-white stylish stouts.
Calmer steeds were never found
Unattached to a merry-go-round.
Equestriennes prefer to jump
Onto horses pillow-plump.

Equestriennes will never ride
As other people do, astride.
They like to balance on one foot,
And wherever they get, they won't stay put.
They utter frequent whoops and yips,
And have the most amazing hips.
Pink seems to be their favorite color,
And very few things are very much duller.

Yet I for one am more than willing
That everything should be less thrilling.
My heart and lungs both bound and balk
When high-wire walkers start to walk.
They ought to perish, yet they don't;
Some fear they will, some fear they won't.

I lack the adjectives, verbs and nouns
To do full justice to the clowns.

Their hearts are constantly breaking, I hear,
And who am I to interfere?
I'd rather shake hands with Mr. Ringling
And tell him his circus is a beautiful thingling.

ONE THIRD OF A CALENDAR

In January everything freezes.
We have two children. Both are she'ses.
This is our January rule:
One girl in bed, and one in school.

In February the blizzard whirls.
We own a pair of little girls.
Blessings upon of each the head —
The one in school and the one in bed.

March is the month of cringe and bluster.
Each of our children has a sister.
They cling together like Hansel and Gretel,
With their noses glued to the benzoin kettle.

April is made of impetuous waters
And doctors looking down throats of daughters.
If we had a son too, and a thoroughbred,
We'd have a horse,
And a boy,
And two girls
In bed.

A CHILD'S GUIDE TO PARENTS

Children, I crave your kind forbearance;
Our topic for today is Parents.

Parents are generally found in couples,
Except when divorce their number quadruples.

Mostly they're married to each other.
The female one is called the mother.

Paternal pride being hard to edit,
The male, or father, claims the credit,

But children, hark! Your mother would rather,
When you arrived, have been your father.

At last on common ground they meet:
Their child is sweetest of the sweet.

But burst not, babe, with boastful glee;
It is themselves they praise, not thee.

The reason Father flatters thee, is —
Thou must be wonderful, aren't thou his?

And Mother admires her offspring double,
Especially after all that trouble.

The wise child handles father and mother
By playing one against the other.

Don't! cries this parent to the tot;
The opposite parent asks, Why not?

Let baby listen, nothing loth,
And work impartially on both.

In clash of wills, do not give in;
Good parents are made by discipline;

Remember the words of the wise old senator:
Spare the tantrum, and spoil the progenitor;

But joy in heaping measure comes
To children whose parents are under their thumbs.

LOW–PRESSURE ARIA

Rain, rain, go away,
Come again another day,
Little Johnny wants to play.

Daddy's just as mad as hops
From looking at the dripping drops,
Daddy doesn't want the rain
To trickle on the windowpane.
Daddy wants an azure sky
And a fairway fast and dry;
He despises sodden turf
And water hazards full of surf.
When he sees a patch of blue
He practices his follow-through;
When the blue reverts to cloud,
Daddy's speech is rude and loud.
Sometimes with an angry shrug
He's putting putts along the rug;

Sometimes figuring out a plan
For murdering the weather man;
In either case it's more than plain
That Daddy doesn't like the rain.

Rain, rain, go away,
Come again another day,
Little Johnny wants to play.

Daddy may be cross, but ah!
Wait until you see Mamma!
She must do without her tennis
When the courts are bits of Venice.
I'm ashamed of what she mutters,
Gazing at the flooded gutters;
I'm afraid that she forgets
It's really raining violets;
That all these little silver drops
Bring the farmer bumper crops.
Mamma is angry when it pours;
She doesn't want to stay indoors.

Rain, rain, go away,
Come again another day,
Little Johnny wants to play.

Silly Johnny doesn't mind
By the weather being confined.
Drawing now, with might and main,
Pictures on the windowpane;
Choosing sides among the drops —
Some are robbers, some are cops.
Silly boy, for days together
He doesn't think about the weather.

I'LL TAKE THE HIGH ROAD COMMISSION

In between the route marks
And the shaving rhymes,
Black and yellow markers
Comment on the times.

All along the highway
Hear the signs discourse:

MEN
SLOW
WORKING
;
SADDLE
CROSSING
HORSE
.

Cryptic crossroad preachers
Proffer good advice,
Helping wary drivers
Keep out of Paradise.

Transcontinental sermons,
Transcendental talk:

SOFT
CAUTION
SHOULDERS
;
CROSS
CHILDREN
WALK
.

[49]

Wisest of the proverbs,
Truest of the talk,
Have I found the dictum:

CROSS
CHILDREN
WALK

.

When Adam took the highway
He left his sons a guide:

CROSS
CHILDREN
WALK

;

CHEERFUL
CHILDREN
RIDE

.

ADVENTURES OF ISABEL

Isabel met an enormous bear,
Isabel, Isabel, didn't care;
The bear was hungry, the bear was ravenous,
The bear's big mouth was cruel and cavernous.
The bear said, Isabel, glad to meet you,
How do, Isabel, now I'll eat you!
Isabel, Isabel, didn't worry,
Isabel didn't scream or scurry.
She washed her hands and she straightened her hair up,
Then Isabel quietly ate the bear up.

[50]

Once in a night as black as pitch
Isabel met a wicked old witch.
The witch's face was cross and wrinkled,
The witch's gums with teeth were sprinkled.
Ho ho, Isabel! the old witch crowed,
I'll turn you into an ugly toad!
Isabel, Isabel, didn't worry,
Isabel didn't scream or scurry,
She showed no rage and she showed no rancor,
But she turned the witch into milk and drank her.

Isabel met a hideous giant,
Isabel continued self-reliant.
The giant was hairy, the giant was horrid,
He had one eye in the middle of his forehead.
Good morning Isabel, the giant said,
I'll grind your bones to make my bread.
Isabel, Isabel, didn't worry,
Isabel didn't scream or scurry.
She nibbled the zwieback that she always fed off,
And when it was gone, she cut the giant's head off.

Isabel met a troublesome doctor,
He punched and he poked till he really shocked her.
The doctor's talk was of coughs and chills
And the doctor's satchel bulged with pills.
The doctor said unto Isabel,
Swallow this, it will make you well.
Isabel, Isabel, didn't worry,
Isabel didn't scream or scurry.
She took those pills from the pill concocter,
And Isabel calmly cured the doctor.

TABLEAU AT TWILIGHT

I sit in the dusk. I am all alone.
Enter a child and an ice-cream cone.

A parent is easily beguiled
By sight of this coniferous child.

The friendly embers warmer gleam,
The cone begins to drip ice cream.

Cones are composed of many a vitamin.
My lap is not the place to bitamin.

Although my raiment is not chinchilla,
I flinch to see it become vanilla.

Coniferous child, when vanilla melts
I'd rather it melted somewhere else.

Exit child with remains of cone.
I sit in the dusk. I am all alone,

Muttering spells like an angry Druid,
Alone, in the dusk, with the cleaning fluid.

EPISTLE TO THE OLYMPIANS

Dear parents, I write you this letter
Because I thought I'd better;
Because I would like to know
Exactly which way to grow.

[52]

My milk I will leave undrunk
If you'd rather have me shrunk,
If your love it will further kindle,
I'll do my best to dwindle;

Or, on the other hand,
Do you wish me to expand?
I'll stuff like a greedy rajah
If you really want me larger.

All that I ask of you
Is to tell me which to do;
To whisper in accents mild
The proper size for a child.

I get so very confused
By the chidings commonly used.
Am I really such a dunce
As to err two ways at once?

When one mood you are in,
My bigness is a sin:
"Oh what a thing to do
For a great big girl like you!"

But then another time
Smallness is my crime:
"Stop doing whatever you're at;
You're far too little for that!"

Kind parents, be so kind
As to kindly make up your mind
And whisper in accents mild
The proper size for a child.

[53]

What am I doing, daughter mine?
A-haying while the sun doth shine;
Gathering rosebuds while I may
To hoard against a barren day;
Reveling in the brief sensation
Of basking in your admiration.
Oh, now, when you are almost five
I am the lordliest man alive;
Your gaze is blind to any flaw,
And brimming with respect and awe.
You think me handsome, strong and brave,
You come at morn to watch me shave.
The neighbors' insults lose their sting
When you encourage me to sing,
And like a fashion plate I pose
While you compliment my clothes.
Who wishes his self-esteem to thrive
Should belong to a girl of almost five.
But almost five can't last forever,
And wide-eyed girls grow tall and clever.
Few creatures others less admire
Than a lass of seventeen her sire.
What humiliation must you weather
When we are seen in public together!
Perchance I'll munch a stick of gum,
Or in the theater brazenly hum;
My hat, I'm sure, will flout the law
Laid down for hats at Old Nassau;
My anecdotes you'll strive to stanch,
And at my table manners blanch;

My every word and every deed
Will agony and embarrassment breed;
Your goal of goals, the end of your ends,
To hide me forever from your friends.
Therefore I now chant roundelays,
And rollick in your pride and praise;
Too soon the nymph that you will be
Will shudder when she looks at me.

THE SNIFFLE

In spite of her sniffle,
Isabel's chiffle.
Some girls with a sniffle
Would be weepy and tiffle;
They would look awful,
Like a rained-on waffle,
But Isabel's chiffle
In spite of her sniffle.
Her nose is more red
With a cold in her head,
But then, to be sure,
Her eyes are bluer.
Some girls with a snuffle,
Their tempers are uffle,
But when Isabel's snivelly
She's snivelly civilly,
And when she is snuffly
She's perfectly luffly.

[55]

SEASIDE SERENADE

It begins when you smell a funny smell,
And it isn't vanilla or caramel,
And it isn't forget-me-nots or lilies,
Or new-mown hay, or daffy-down-dillies,
And it's not what the barber rubs on Father,
And it's awful, and yet you like it rather.
No, it's not what the barber rubs on Daddy,
It's more like an elderly finnan haddie,
Or, shall we say, an electric fan
Blowing over a sardine can.
It's as fishy as millions of fishy fishes,
In spite of which you find it delishes,
You could do with a second helping, please,
And that, my dears, is the ocean breeze.
And pretty soon you observe a pack
Of people reclining upon their back,
And another sight that is very common
Is people reclining upon their abdomen.
And now you lose the smell of the ocean
In the sweetish vapor of sunburn lotion,
And the sun itself seems paler and colder,
Compared to vermilion face and shoulder.
Athletic young men uncover their torso
In the virile way that maidens adore so,
While paunchy uncles, before they bathe them,
In voluminous beach robes modestly swathe them.
The beach is peppered with ladies who look
Like pictures out of a medical book.
Last, not least, consider the kiddies,
Chirping like crickets and katydiddies,

Splashing, squealing, slithering, crawling,
Cheerful, tearful, boisterous, bawling,
Kiddies in clamorous crowds that swarm
Heavily over your prostrate form,
Kiddies who bring, as a priceless cup,
Something dead that a wave washed up.
Oh, I must go down to the beach, my lass,
And step on a piece of broken glass.

PIANO TUNER, UNTUNE ME THAT TUNE

I regret that before people can be reformed they have to be
    sinners,
And that before you have pianists in the family you have
    to have beginners.
When it comes to beginners' music
I am not enthusic,
And when listening to something called "An Evening in
    My Doll House," or "The Bee and the Clover,"
Why I'd like just once to hear it played all the way through,
    instead of that hard part near the end over and
    over.
Have you noticed about little fingers?
When they hit a sour note, they lingers.
And another thing about little fingers, they are always
    strawberry-jammed or cranberry-jellied-y,
And "Chopsticks" is their favorite melody,
And if there is one man who I hope his dentist was a
    sadist and all his teeth were brittle ones,
It is he who invented "Chopsticks" for the little ones.
My good wishes are less than frugal

For him who started the little ones going boogie-woogal,
But for him who started the little ones picking out "Chopsticks" on the ivories,
Well I wish him a thousand harems of a thousand wives
apiece, and a thousand little ones by each wife, and
each little one playing "Chopsticks" twenty-four hours
a day in all the nurseries of all his harems, or
wiveries.

TRICK OR TREK

If my face is white as a newmade sail,
It's not that it's clean, it's simply pale.
The reason it's pale as well as clean:
I'm a shaken survivor of Hallowe'en.
The little ones of our community
This year passed up no opportunity;
You should have seen the goblins and witches;
At our expense, they were all in stitches.
They shook with snickers from warp to woof
When our doormat landed on the roof.
And take a look at our garden's format —
It now resembles the missing doormat.
The doorbell got torn out by the roots,
So our guests announce themselves tooting flutes.
Don't blame me if I wince or flinch,
They tore the fence down inch by inch.
Forgive me if I flinch or wince,
We haven't seen our mailbox since,
And we can't get into our own garage
Since they gave the door that Swedish massage.

All this perhaps I could forgive,
In loving kindness I might live,
But on every window they scrawled in soap
Those deathless lines, *Mr. Nash is a dope.*
At the very glimpse of a jack-o'-lantern
I've got one foot on the bus to Scranton.
When Hallowe'en next delivers the goods,
You may duck for apples — I'll duck for the woods.

ASK DADDY, HE WON'T KNOW

Now that they've abolished chrome work
I'd like to call their attention to home work.
Here it is only three decades since my scholarship was
   famous,
And I'm an ignoramus.
I cannot think which goes sideways and which goes up
   and down, a parallel or a meridian,
Nor do I know the name of him who first translated the
   Bible into Indian, I see him only as an enterprising
   colonial Gideon.
I have difficulty with dates,
To say nothing of the annual rainfall of the Southern Cen-
   tral States,
And the only way I can distinguish proper from improper
   fractions
Is by their actions.
Naturally the correct answers are just back of the tip of my
   tongue,
But try to explain that to your young.
I am overwhelmed by their erudite banter,

I am in no condition to differentiate between Tamerlane
    and Tam o' Shanter.
I reel, I sway, I am utterly exhausted;
Should you ask me when Chicago was founded I could
    only reply I didn't even know it was losted.

SOLILOQUY IN CIRCLES

Being a father
Is quite a bother.

You are free as air
With time to spare,

You're a fiscal rocket
With change in your pocket,

And then one morn
A child is born.

Your life has been runcible,
Irresponsible,

Like an arrow or javelin
You've been constantly travelin',

But mostly, I daresay,
Without a *chaise percée*,

To which by comparison
Nothing's embarison.

But all children matures,
Maybe even yours.

You improve them mentally
And straighten them dentally,

They grow tall as a lancer
And ask questions you can't answer,

And supply you with data
About how everybody else wears lipstick sooner and stays
    up later,

And if they are popular,
The phone they monopular.

They scorn the dominion
Of their parent's opinion,

They're no longer corralable
Once they find that you're fallible.

But after you've raised them and educated them and
    gowned them,
They just take their little fingers and wrap you around
    them.

Being a father
Is quite a bother,
But I like it, rather.

THERE'S NOTHING LIKE INSTINCT, FORTUNATELY

I suppose that plumbers' children know more about plumb-
    ing than plumbers do, and welders' children more
    about welding than welders,
Because the only fact in an implausible world is that all
    young know better than their elders.
A young person is a person with nothing to learn,
One who already knows that ice does not chill and fire does
    not burn.
It knows that it can read indefinitely in the dark and do its
    eyes no harm,
It knows it can climb on the back of a thin chair to look
    for a sweater it left on the bus without falling and
    breaking an arm.
It knows it can spend six hours in the sun on its first day at
    the beach without ending up a skinless beet,
And it knows it can walk barefoot through the barn with-
    out running a nail in its feet.
It knows it doesn't need a raincoat if it's raining or galoshes
    if it's snowing,
And knows how to manage a boat without ever having done
    any sailing or rowing.
It knows that it is an expert, not a beginner,
And that its appetite is not affected by eating three choco-
    late bars covered with peanut butter and guava jelly,
    fifteen minutes before dinner.
Most of all it knows
That only other people catch colds through sitting around
    in drafts in wet clothes.

Meanwhile psychologists grow rich
Writing that the young are ones parents should not under-
    mine the self-confidence of which.

TARKINGTON, THOU SHOULD'ST BE
LIVING IN THIS HOUR

O Adolescence, O Adolescence,
I wince before thine incandescence.
Thy constitution young and hearty
Is too much for this aged party.
Thou standest with loafer-flattened feet
Where bras and funny papers meet.
When anxious elders swarm about
Crying "Where are you going?" thou answerest "Out,"
Leaving thy parents swamped in debts
For bubble gum and cigarettes.

Thou spurnest in no uncertain tone
The sirloin for the ice-cream cone;
Not milk, but cola, is thy potion;
Thou wearest earrings in the ocean,
Blue jeans at dinner, or maybe shorts,
And lipstick on the tennis courts.

Forever thou whisperest, two by two,
Of who is madly in love with who.
The car thou needest every day,
Let hub caps scatter where they may.
For it would start unfriendly talk
If friends should chance to see thee walk.

Friends! Heavens, how they come and go!
Best pal today, tomorrow foe,
Since to distinguish thou dost fail
Twixt confidante and tattletale,
And blanchest to find the beach at noon
With sacred midnight secrets strewn.

Strewn! All is lost and nothing found.
Lord, how thou leavest things around!
Sweaters and rackets in the stable,
And purse upon the drugstore table,
And cameras rusting in the rain,
And Daddy's patience down the drain.

Ah well, I must not carp and cavil,
I'll chew the spinach, spit out the gravel,
Remembering how my heart has leapt
At times when me thou didst accept.
Still, I'd like to be present, I must confess,
When thine own adolescents adolesce.

A CAROL FOR CHILDREN

God rest you, merry Innocents,
Let nothing you dismay,
Let nothing wound an eager heart
Upon this Christmas day.

Yours be the genial holly wreaths,
The stockings and the tree;
An aged world to you bequeaths
Its own forgotten glee.

[64]

Soon, soon enough come crueler gifts,
The anger and the tears;
Between you now there sparsely drifts
A handful yet of years.

Oh, dimly, dimly glows the star
Through the electric throng;
The bidding in temple and bazaar
Drowns out the silver song.

The ancient altars smoke afresh,
The ancient idols stir;
Faint in the reek of burning flesh
Sink frankincense and myrrh.

Gaspar, Balthazar, Melchior!
Where are your offerings now?
What greetings to the Prince of War,
His darkly branded brow?

Two ultimate laws alone we know,
The ledger and the sword —
So far away, so long ago,
We lost the infant Lord.

Only the children clasp his hand;
His voice speaks low to them,
And still for them the shining band
Wings over Bethlehem.

God rest you, merry Innocents,
While innocence endures.
A sweeter Christmas than we to ours
May you bequeath to yours.

DADDY, I WANT A PET FOR MY VERY OWN, I PROMISE TO TAKE CARE OF IT

THE OCTOPUS

Tell me, O Octopus, I begs,
Is those things arms, or is they legs?
I marvel at thee, Octopus;
If I were thou, I'd call me Us.

HOMEWARD BUND

Be careful not to hate the moth,
It isn't she who eats your cloth,
But only little ones of hers
That lunch on tweeds and dine on furs.
Who but a Scrooge his heart could steel
To spray these gamins out of a meal?
My heart is mush, so come on, larvæ,
My closet's full, and I'm Fred Harvey.

GLOSSINA MORSITANS, OR, THE TSETSE

Aunt Betsy was fixing to change her will,
And would have left us out in the chill.
A *Glossina morsitans* bit Aunt Betsy.
Tsk tsk, tsetse.

THE CAMEL

The camel has a single hump;
The dromedary, two;
Or else the other way around.
I'm never sure. Are you?

[69]

THE PIG

The pig, if I am not mistaken,
Supplies us sausage, ham, and bacon.
Let others say his heart is big —
I call it stupid of the pig.

THE POULTRIES

Let's think of eggs.
They have no legs.
Chickens come from eggs
But they have legs.
The plot thickens;
Eggs come from chickens,
But have no legs under 'em.
What a conundrum!

THE LAMB

Little gamboling lamb,
Do you know where you am?
In a patch of mint.
I'll give you a hint.
Scram,
Lamb!

THE SEA–GULL

Hark to the whimper of the sea-gull;
He weeps because he's not an ea-gull.
Suppose you were, you silly sea-gull,
Could you explain it to your she-gull?

[70]

THE GERM

A mighty creature is the germ,
Though smaller than the pachyderm.
His customary dwelling place
Is deep within the human race.
His childish pride he often pleases
By giving people strange diseases.
Do you, my poppet, feel infirm?
You probably contain a germ.

THE GUPPY

Whales have calves,
Cats have kittens,
Bears have cubs,
Bats have bittens.
Swans have cygnets,
Seals have puppies,
But guppies just have little guppies.

THE COW

The cow is of the bovine ilk;
One end is moo, the other, milk.

THE RHINOCEROS

The rhino is a homely beast,
For human eyes he's not a feast.
Farewell, farewell, you old rhinoceros,
I'll stare at something less prepoceros.

[71]

THE EEL

I don't mind eels
Except as meals.
And the way they feels.

THE PHŒNIX

Deep in the study
Of eugenics
We find that fabled
Fowl, the Phœnix.
The wisest bird
As ever was,
Rejecting other
Mas and Pas,
It lays one egg,
Not ten or twelve,
And when it's hatched,
Out pops itselve.

THE WOMBAT

The wombat lives across the seas,
Among the far Antipodes.
He may exist on nuts and berries,
Or then again, on missionaries;
His distant habitat precludes
Conclusive knowledge of his moods.
But I would not engage the wombat
In any form of mortal combat.

THE SHREW

Strange as it seems, the smallest mammal
Is the shrew, and not the camel.
And that is all I ever knew,
Or wish to know, about the shrew.

I HAPPEN TO KNOW

Hark to the locusts in their shrill armadas.
Locusts aren't locusts. Locusts are cicadas.

To seals in circuses I travel on bee lines.
Seals aren't seals. Seals are sea lions.

I'm a buffalo hunter. Want to see my license?
Buffaloes aren't buffaloes. Buffaloes are bisons.

I'm too old to be pedantically hocus-pocused.
I'll stand on the buffalo, the seal and the locust.

THE SKINK

Let us do justice to the skink
Who isn't what so many think.
On consultation with a wizard
I find the skink a kind of lizard.
Since he is not a printer's whim,
Don't sniff and back away from him.
Or you may be adjudged too drunk
To tell a lizard from a skunk.

THE SMELT

Oh, why does man pursue the smelt?
It has no valuable pelt,
It boasts of no escutcheon royal,
It yields no ivory or oil,
Its life is dull, its death is tame,
A fish as humble as its name.
Yet — take this salmon somewhere else.
And bring me half a dozen smelts.

CREEPS AND CRAWLS

The insect world appealed to Fabre.
I find the insect world macabre.
In every hill of ants I see
A governed glimpse of what shall be,
And sense in every web contriver
Man's predecessor and survivor.
Someday, perhaps, my citronella
Will rank with Chamberlain's umbrella.

THE JELLYFISH

Who wants my jellyfish?
I'm not sellyfish!

THE GANDER

Be careful not to cross the gander,
A bird composed of beak and dander.
His heart is filled with prideful hate
Of all the world except his mate,
And if the neighbors do not err
He's overfond of beating her.
Is she happy? What's the use
Of trying to psychoanalyze a goose?

THE GRACKLE

The grackle's voice is less than mellow,
His heart is black, his eye is yellow,
He bullies more attractive birds
With hoodlum deeds and vulgar words,
And should a human interfere,
Attacks that human in the rear.
I cannot help but deem the grackle
An ornithological debacle.

THE PORPOISE

I kind of like the playful porpoise,
A healthy mind in a healthy corpus.
He and his cousin, the playful dolphin,
Why they like swimmin like I like golphin.

THE FIREFLY

The firefly's flame
Is something for which science has no name.
I can think of nothing eerier
Than flying around with an unidentified glow on a person's posteerier.

THE SHARK

How many scientists have written
The shark is gentle as a kitten!
Yet this I know about the shark:
His bite is worser than his bark.

THE WASP

The wasp and all his numerous family
I look upon as a major calamily.
He throws open his nest with prodigality,
But I distrust his waspitality.

THE SQUIRREL

A squirrel to some is a squirrel,
To others, a squirrel's a squirl.
Since freedom of speech is the birthright of each,
I can only this fable unfurl:
A virile young squirrel named Cyril,

In an argument over a girl,
Was lambasted from here to the Tyrol
By a churl of a squirl named Earl.

THE FLY

The Lord in His wisdom made the fly
And then forgot to tell us why.

THE TERMITE

Some primal termite knocked on wood
And tasted it, and found it good,
And that is why your Cousin May
Fell through the parlor floor today.

THE TURKEY

There is nothing more perky
Than a masculine turkey.
When he struts he struts
With no ifs or buts.
When his face is apoplectic
His harem grows hectic,
And when he gobbles
Their universe wobbles.

THE PORCUPINE

Any hound a porcupine nudges
Can't be blamed for harboring grudges.
I know one hound that laughed all winter
At a porcupine that sat on a splinter.

THE PANTHER

The panther is like a leopard,
Except it hasn't been peppered.
Should you behold a panther crouch,
Prepare to say Ouch.
Better yet, if called by a panther,
Don't anther.

THE CALF

Pray, butcher, spare yon tender calf!
Accept my plea on his behalf;
He's but a babe, too young by far
To perish in the abattoir.
Oh, cruel butcher, let him feed
And gambol on the verdant mead;
Let clover tops and grassy banks
Fill out those childish ribs and flanks.
Then may we, at some future meal,
Pitch into beef, instead of veal.

THE PURIST

I give you now Professor Twist,
A conscientious scientist.
Trustees exclaimed, "He never bungles!"
And sent him off to distant jungles.
Camped on a tropic riverside,
One day he missed his loving bride.
She had, the guide informed him later,
Been eaten by an alligator.
Professor Twist could not but smile.
"You mean," he said, "a crocodile."

THE KITTEN

The trouble with a kitten is
THAT
Eventually it becomes a
CAT.

THE LION

Oh, weep for Mr. and Mrs. Bryan!
He was eaten by a lion;
Following which, the lion's lioness
Up and swallowed Bryan's Bryaness.

THE DUCK

Behold the duck.
It does not cluck.
A cluck it lacks.
It quacks.
It is specially fond
Of a puddle or pond.
When it dines or sups,
It bottoms ups.

THE CANARY

The song of canaries
Never varies,
And when they're moulting
They're pretty revolting.

THE LAMA

The one-l lama,
He's a priest.
The two-l llama,
He's a beast.
And I will bet
A silk pajama
There isn't any
Three-l lllama.*

* The author's attention has been called to a type of conflagration known as a three-alarmer. Pooh.

THE ANT

The ant has made himself illustrious
Through constant industry industrious.
So what?
Would you be calm and placid
If you were full of formic acid?

THE HIPPOPOTAMUS

Behold the hippopotamus!
We laugh at how he looks to us,
And yet in moments dank and grim
I wonder how we look to him.
Peace, peace, thou hippopotamus!
We really look all right to us,
As you no doubt delight the eye
Of other hippopotami.

THE CENTIPEDE

I objurgate the centipede,
A bug we do not really need.
At sleepy-time he beats a path
Straight to the bedroom or the bath.
You always wallop where he's not,
Or, if he is, he makes a spot.

PART THREE

AROUND THE HOUSE

OR

WHAT PARENTS THINK ABOUT WHEN THEY AREN'T THINKING ABOUT CHILDREN

WHAT ALMOST EVERY WOMAN KNOWS
SOONER OR LATER

Husbands are things that wives have to get used to putting
   up with,
And with whom they breakfast with and sup with.
They interfere with the discipline of nurseries,
And forget anniversaries,
And when they have been particularly remiss
They think they can cure everything with a great big kiss.
They are annoying when they stay home
And even more annoying when they roam,
And when you tell them about something they have done
   they just look unbearably patient and smile a superior
   smile,
And think, Oh she'll get over it after a while.
And when it's a question of walking five miles to play golf
   they are very energetic but if it's doing anything useful
   around the house they are very lethargic,
And then they tell you that women are unreasonable and
   don't know anything about logic,
And they never want to go to the same show or listen to the
   same program that you do,
And when you perform some simple rite like putting cold
   cream on your face they seem to think you are up to
   some kind of black magic or Voodoo,
And they are brave and calm and cool and collected about
   the ailments of the person they have promised to honor
   and cherish,
But the minute they get a sniffle or a stomach-ache of their
   own, why you'd think they were about to perish,
And when you are alone with them they ignore all the

minor courtesies and as for airs and graces, they utterly
lack them,

But when there are a lot of people around they hand you
so many chairs and ash trays and sandwiches and
butter you with such bowings and scrapings that you
want to smack them.

Husbands are indeed an irritating form of life,

And yet through some quirk of Providence most of them
are really very deeply ensconced in the affection of
their wife.

I WILL ARISE AND GO NOW

In far Tibet
There live a lama,
He got no poppa,
Got no momma,

He got no wife,
He got no chillun,
Got no use
For penicillun,

He got no soap,
He got no opera,
He don't know Irium
From copra,

He got no songs,
He got no banter,
Don't know Jolson,
Don't know Cantor,

He got no teeth,
He got no gums,
Don't eat no Spam,
Don't need no Tums.

He love to nick him
When he shave;
He also got
No hair to save.

Got no distinction,
No clear head,
Don't call for Calvert;
Drink milk instead.

He use no lotions
For allurance,
He got no car
And no insurance,

He live just like
The lower mammals,
Got no sore throat
From not smoking Camels.

No Winchell warnings,
No Pearson rumor
For this self-centered
Nonconsumer.

Indeed, the
Ignorant Have-Not

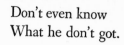

Don't even know
What he don't got.

If you will mind
The box-tops, comma,
I think I'll go
And join that lama.

LINES TO A WORLD–FAMOUS POET WHO FAILED TO COMPLETE A WORLD–FAMOUS POEM

OR

COME CLEAN, MR. GUEST!

Oft when I'm sitting without anything to read waiting for a train in a depot,

I torment myself with the poet's dictum that to make a house a home, livin' is what it takes a heap o'.

Now, I myself should very much enjoy makin' my house a home, but my brain keeps on a-goin' clickety-click, clickety-click, clickety-click,

If Peter Piper picked a peck o' heap o' livin', what kind of a peck o' heap o' livin' would Peter Piper pick?

Certainly a person doesn't need the brains of a Lincoln

To know that there are many kinds o' livin', just as there are many kinds o' dancin' or huntin' or fishin' or eatin' or drinkin'.

A philosophical poet should be specific

As well as prolific,

And I trust I am not being offensive

If I suggest that he should also be comprehensive.

[88]

You may if you like verify my next statement by sending
a stamped, self-addressed envelope to either Dean Inge
or Dean Gauss,

But meanwhile I ask you to believe that it takes a heap of
other things besides a heap o' livin' to make a home
out of a house.

To begin with, it takes a heap o' payin',

And you don't pay just the oncet, but agayin and agayin
and agayin.

Buyin' a stock is called speculatin' and buyin' a house is
called investin',

But the value of the stock or of the house fluctuates up and
down, generally down, just as an irresponsible Destiny
may destine.

Something else that your house takes a heap o', whether the
builder came from Sicily or Erin,

Is repairin',

In addition to which, gentle reader, I am sorry to say you
are little more than an imbecile or a cretin

If you think it doesn't take a heap o' heatin',

And unless you're spiritually allied to the little Dutch boy
who went around inspectin' dikes lookin' for leaks to
put his thumb in,

It takes a heap o' plumbin',

And if it's a house that you're hopin' to spend not just today
but tomorrow in,

It takes a heap o' borrowin'.

In a word, Macushla,

There's a scad o' things that to make a house a home it
takes not only a heap, or a peck, but at least a bushela.

AN INTRODUCTION TO DOGS

The dog is man's best friend.
He has a tail on one end.
Up in front he has teeth.
And four legs underneath.

Dogs like to bark.
They like it best after dark.
They not only frighten prowlers away
But also hold the sandman at bay.

A dog that is indoors
To be let out implores.
You let him out and what then?
He wants back in again.

Dogs display reluctance and wrath
If you try to give them a bath.
They bury bones in hideaways
And half the time they trot sideaways.

They cheer up people who are frowning,
And rescue people who are drowning,
They also track mud on beds,
And chew people's clothes to shreds.

Dogs in the country have fun.
They run and run and run.
But in the city this species
Is dragged around on leashes.

Dogs are upright as a steeple
And much more loyal than people.
Well people may be reprehensibler
But I still think they are sensibler,
Because as Mr. Benchley found,
They can lie down without turning three times around.

THE MIDDLE OF THE MONTH

Oh, some people grieve for New Year's Eve,
And some for the dog days fiddle;
My moment sublime is the restful time
When the month is at the middle.

Sing tirra lirra loo for the middle of the month,
Which wipes out woes like chamois!
The middle of the month is honey and milk!
The middle of the month is mammy!
Now let us exult,
For the bills of ult.
Are limbo's laughing stocks;
At Fate we scoff,
For a fortnight off
Are the impotent bills of prox.
The first of the month is oyster-gray,
The last of the month is clammy,
But it's tirra lirra loo for the middle of the month,
For the middle of the month is mammy!

Time, fly not back upon thy track!
The past is merely tedium,

[91]

And the future, too; so stand still, do,
While the month is at the medium!

Then tirra lirra loo for the middle of the month
And gambol it in like May Day!
The ravenous wolves are toothless now,
The lambs are in their heyday.
Now turn not pale
At the morning mail
Nor shrink when the telephone shrills,
No evil betides
On the blessed Ides,
The lull between the bills!
Oh, the first of the month is oyster-gray
And the last of the month is clammy,
But it's tirra lirra loo for the middle of the month,
For the middle of the month is mammy!

MACHINERY DOESN'T ANSWER, EITHER, BUT YOU AREN'T MARRIED TO IT

Oh, Daddy, look at that man, excuse my pointing, but just
    look at him!
He is in a frenzy or something, as if a red rag or something
    had been shook at him!
His eyes are rolling like a maniac's,
Oh, isn't it shocking how insaniacs!
Oh, Daddy, he is talking to thin air,
He is having a long conversation with somebody who isn't
    there!
He is talking to himself, he must be under the influence of
    either Luna or Bacchus;

Oh, Daddy, Daddy, I think we had better go a long way
away from him immediately because one in his condition might at any moment have an impulse to attac-
chus!

Nay, hush ye, hush ye, do not fret ye, my little white man-
child,

Who if your parents hadn't been Caucasian would have
been an ebony or copper or tan child,

Draw nigh and harken

While I your mind enlighten or undarken.

Life will teach you many things, chief of which is that
every man who talks to himself isn't necessarily out of
his wits;

He may have a wife who knits.

Probably only he and his Maker

Know how many evenings he has spent trying to raise a
conversation while his beloved created dresses and
sweaters by the acre.

Ah, my inquiring offspring, you must learn that life can
be very bitter,

But never quite so much so as when trying to pry a word
out of a knitter.

Sometimes she knits and sits,

Sometimes she sits and knits,

And you tell her what you have been doing all day and you
ask what she has been doing all day and nothing
happens, and you tell her what you would like to
do this evening and ask her what she would like
to do this evening and nothing happens, and you
think you will disintegrate if you don't get some response, and you speak tenderly of your courtship and
your bridal,

And you might just as well try to get a response out of an
    Oriental idol,
And you notice a spasmodic movement of her lips,
And you think she is going to say something but she is only
    counting the number of stitches it takes to surround
    the hips;
And she furrows her beautiful brow, which is a sign that
    something is wrong somewhere, and you keep on talk-
    ing and disregard the sign,
And she casts a lethal glance, as one who purls before swine,
And you can tantrum your best tantrums and wheedle your
    best wheedles,
But you can't compete with the hypnotic needles,
And this goes on for weeks
At the end of which she lays her work down and speaks,
And you think now maybe you can have some home life
    but she speaks in a tone as far off as Mercury or
    Saturn,
And she says thank goodness that is finished, it is a sight
    and she will never be able to wear it, but it doesn't
    matter because she can hardly wait to start on an
    adorable new pattern,
And when this has been going on for a long time, why
    that's the time that strong men break down and go
    around talking to themselves in public, finally,
And it doesn't mean that they are weak mentally or spi-
    nally,
It doesn't mean, my boy, that they ought to be in an asylum
    like Nijinsky the dancer,
It only means that they got into the habit of talking to them-
    selves at home because they themselves were the only
    people they could talk to and get an answer.

I'LL GET ONE TOMORROW

Barber, barber, come and get me;
Hairy torrents irk and fret me.
Hair and hair again appears,
And climbs like ivy round my ears;
Hair across my collar gambols;
Down my neck it wayward ambles;
Ever down it trips and trickles,
Yes, and where it trips, it tickles.
Barber dear, I wish I knew
Why I do not visit you,
Why I grudge the minutes ten
In your sanitary den,
Why I choose to choke on hair
Rather than to mount your chair.
Men no busier than I
Weekly to your office hie;
Men no braver than myself
Confront the armory on your shelf;
Men no wealthier than me
Gladly meet your modest fee,
And for a fraction of a dollar
Keep the jungle off their collar.
I alone am shy and flustered,
A solitary, cowardly custard,
Shaggy as a prize Angora,
Overrun with creeping flora.
Barber, barber, you're in luck;
The bell has rung, the hour has struck.
Sloth is strong, but hair is stronger;
I cannot stand it any longer.

Barber, barber, here I come;
Shake up the odorous bay rum;
Bring on your shears, your scythes, your snippers,
Bring on your crisp, electric clippers;
Employ a dozen extra sweepers;
Bring giant harvesters and reapers;
I warn you that a bumper crop
Waits to overwhelm your shop.
Barber, barber, be verbose,
Be anything, but clip me close;
Leave me razored, leave me scissored.
Leave me hairless as a lizard;
Barber, barber, singe and scald;
Barber, can't you make me bald?
I'd be the happiest of men,
And never think of you again.

ABDICATION OF A JESTER

Once there was a man and he wasn't famous for his clothes,
He was famous for his *bon mots*.
Dinner parties waited hungrily if he didn't come in till late
Because they could count on him to scintillate;
Just give him a cocktail or two to relax him
And you would be repaid with an epigram or a maxim;
He was invariably original,
And he did not have to depend for his effect on the in-
    delicate or sacrileginal;
Of quips and anecdotes he was a warehouse,
And everybody wanted him at their house.
Yes indeed, he was quite a wit,

And then one day he suddenly quit.

He seldom went out and when he did go out he seldom opened his mouth,

And when he did, it was only to remark on the current blizzard or flood or drouth;

On scintillation he clamped down a total embargo,

And his most stimulating remark to a dinner partner in three months was, So you're from Louisville, I used to know some people named Perkins in Louisville, but it seems to me I heard they'd moved to Chicago.

And at first everybody was patient but at last their brows grew darkling,

And they went to him and said, Look here, how about a little sparkling?

And he said, Do you see these lips?

And they said they did, and he said, Well they shall never more be crossed by wanton wiles and cranks and quips.

He said, I have spent my life studying the fundamentals of wit and humor and table talk,

I have spent a fortune in time and effort to master the art of stimulating and able talk;

To every aphorism of mine you ever quoted,

Why, years of experience were devoted,

And then, he said, and then the baby is told to speak to Mr. Katz the grocer on the telephone, Go ahead, baby, speak to Mr. Katz, and the baby says Meow,

And the spasms of mirth raised by baby's repartee still echo in my ears right now.

No, he said, hereafter count me not a wit, count me simply a good neighbor.

I am too old and proud to compete with unskilled labor.

THE PARTY

Come Arabella, fetch the cake,
On a dish with silver handles.
Oh mercy! Feel the table shake!
Lucinda, light the candles.

For Mr. Migg is thir–ty,
Is thir——ty,
Is thir———ty.
The years are crawling over him
Like wee red ants.
Oh, three times ten is thir–ty,
Is for——ty,
Is fif———ty.
The further off from England
The nearer is to France.

The little flames they bob and jig,
The dining hall is breezy.
Quick! puff your candles, Mr. Migg,
The little flames die easy.
For Mr. Migg is for–ty,
Is for——ty,
Is for———ty.
The years are crawling over him
Like wee red ants.
Oh four times ten is for–ty,
Is fif——ty,
Is six———ty,
And creeping through the icing,
The other years advance.

Why, Arabella, here's a ring!
Lucinda, here's a thimble!
For Mr. Migg there's not a thing —
'Tis not, I trust, a symbol!

For Mr. Migg is fif–ty,
Is fif——ty,
Is fif———ty.
The years are crawling over him
Like wee red ants.
Oh, five times ten is fif–ty,
Is six——ty,
Is seven———ty.
Lucinda, put the cake away.
We're going to the dance.

THE STRANGE CASE OF MR. ORMANTUDE'S BRIDE

Once there was a bridegroom named Mr. Ormantude whose
    intentions were hard to disparage,
Because he intended to make his a happy marriage,
And he succeeded for going on fifty years,
During which he was in marital bliss up to his ears.
His wife's days and nights were enjoyable
Because he catered to every foible;
He went around humming hymns
And anticipating her whims.
Many a fine bit of repartee died on his lips
Lest it throw her anecdotes into eclipse;
He was always silent when his cause was meritorious,

And he never engaged in argument unless sure he was so
obviously wrong that she couldn't help emerging vic-
torious,
And always when in her vicinity
He was careful to make allowances for her femininity;
Were she snappish, he was sweetish,
And of understanding her he made a fetish.
Everybody said his chances of celebrating his golden wed-
ding looked good,
But on his golden wedding eve he was competently poi-
soned by his wife who could no longer stand being
perpetually understood.

"TOMORROW, PARTLY CLOUDY"

Rainy vacations
Try people's patience.
To expect rain in the autumn
Experience has tautumn,
And rain in the spring and winter
Makes no stories for the printer,
But rain on summer colonies
Breeds misdemeanors and felonies.
Summer cottages are meant just to sleep in,
Not to huddle all day in a heap in,
And whether at sea level or in higher places
There are not enough fireplaces,
And the bookcase stares at you starkly
And seems to be full of nothing but Volume II of the *Life
of Rutherford B. Hayes,* and *The Rosary,* by Florence
M. Barclay,

And everybody wishes they had brought woolens and
    tweeds instead of linens and foulards,
And if you succeed in lining up four for bridge the only
    deck turns out to have only fifty-one cards,
And tennis rackets grow frazzled and golf sticks rusty and
    bathing suits moldy,
And parents grow scoldy,
And on all sides you hear nothing but raindrops going
    sputter-sput, sputter-sput,
And bureau drawers won't open and bathroom doors won't
    shut,
And all attempts at amusement fail,
Even reading the previous tenants' jettisoned mail,
Although naturally it would never have been jettisoned
If it hadn't been reticent.
But you could stand everything if it wasn't for one ma-
    lignant committee,
Which is the one that turns the sun on again just as you are
    leaving for the city.
Yes indeed, rainy vacations
Certainly try people's patience.

SUPPOSE HE THREW IT IN YOUR FACE

Please don't anybody ask me to decide anything, I do not
    know a nut from a meg,
Or which came first, the lady or the tiger, or which came
    next, the chicken or the egg.
It takes a man of vision
To make a decision.
I am, alas, to be reckoned

With the shortstop who can't decide whether to throw to
      first or second,
And where this twilight mind really goes into eclipse
Is in the matter of tips.
I stand stricken before the triple doom,
Whether, and How Much, and Whom.
Tell me, which is more unpleasant,
The look from him who is superior to a tip and gets it, or
      from him who isn't and doesn't?
I had rather be discovered playing with my toes in the
      Boston Aquarium
Than decide wrongly about an honorarium.
Oh, to dwell forever amid Utopian scenery
Where hotels and restaurants and service stations are oper-
      ated by untippable unoffendable machinery!

PLEASE PASS THE BISCUIT

I have a little dog,
Her name is Spangle.
And when she eats
I think she'll strangle.

She's darker than Hamlet,
Lighter than Porgy;
Her heart is gold,
Her odor, dorgy.

Her claws click-click
Across the floor,
Her nose is always
Against a door.

The squirrel flies
Her pursuing mouth;
Should he fly north,
She pursues him south.

Yet do not mock her
As she hunts;
Remember, she caught
A milkman once.

Like liquid gems
Her eyes burn clearly;
She's five years old,
And house-trained, nearly.

Her shame is deep
When she has erred;
She dreads the blow
Less than the word.

I marvel that such
Small ribs as these
Can cage such vast
Desire to please.

She's as much a part
Of the house as the mortgage,
Spangle, I wish you
A ripe old dortgage.

Oh, early every afternoon
I like a temporary swoon.
I do not overeat at luncheon,
I do not broach the bowl or puncheon;
Yet the hour from two to three
Is always sleepy-time to me.

Bolt upright at my desk I sit,
My elbows digging into it,
My chin into my hands doth fit,
My careful fingers screen my eyes,
And all my work before me lies,
Which leads inquisitive passer-bys
Who glance my way and see me nod,
To think me wide awake, if odd.

I would not sell my daily swoon
For all the rubies in Rangoon.
What! sell my swoon? My lovely swoon?
Oh, many and many's the afternoon
I've scoured the woods with Daniel Boone,
And sipped a julep with Lorna Doone
And former Governor Ruby Laffoon.
I'll sell my soul before my swoon,
It's not for sale, my swoon's immune.

From two to three each afternoon
Mine are the mountains of the moon,
Mine a congenital silver spoon.
And I can lead a lost platoon
Or dive for pearls in a haunted lagoon,

Or guide a stratosphere balloon.
Oh, where the schooner schoons, I schoon,
I can talk lion, or baboon,
Or make a crooner cease to croon.
I like to swoon, for when I swoon
The universe is my macaroon.
Then blessings on thee, my afternoon torpor,
Thou makest a prince of a mental porpor.

WE DON'T NEED TO LEAVE YET, DO WE?
OR, YES WE DO

One kind of person when catching a train always wants to
   allow an hour to cover the ten-block trip to the termi-
   nus,
And the other kind looks at them as if they were vermi-
   nous,
And the second kind says that five minutes is plenty and
   will even leave one minute over for buying the tickets,
And the first kind looks at them as if they had cerebral
   rickets.
One kind when theater-bound sups lightly at six and
   hastens off to the play,
And indeed I know one such person who is so such that it
   frequently arrives in time for the last act of the
   matinee,
And the other kind sits down at eight to a meal that is
   positively sumptuous,
Observing cynically that an eight-thirty curtain never rises
   till eight-forty, an observation which is less cynical
   than bumptuous.

And what the first kind, sitting uncomfortably in the wait-
    ing room while the train is made up in the yards, can
    never understand,
Is the injustice of the second kind's reaching their seat just
    as the train moves out, just as they had planned,
And what the second kind cannot understand as they
    stumble over the first kind's feet just as the footlights
    flash on at last
Is that the first kind doesn't feel the least bit foolish at
    having entered the theater before the cast.
Oh, the first kind always wants to start now and the second
    kind always wants to tarry,
Which wouldn't make any difference, except that each
    other is what they always marry.

POLTERGUEST, MY POLTERGUEST

I've put Miss Hopper upon the train,
And I hope to do so never again,
For must I do so, I shouldn't wonder
If, instead of upon it, I put her under.

Never has host encountered a visitor
Less desirabler, less exquisiter,
Or experienced such a tangy zest
In beholding the back of a parting guest.

Hoitiful-toitiful Hecate Hopper
Haunted our house and haunted it proper,
Hecate Hopper left the property
Irredeemably Hecate Hopperty.

The morning paper was her monopoly
She read it first, and Hecate Hopperly,
Handing on to the old subscriber
A wad of Dorothy Dix and fiber.

Shall we coin a phrase for "to unco-operate"?
How about trying "to Hecate Hopperate"?
On the maid's days off she found it fun
To breakfast in bed at quarter to one.

Not only was Hecate on a diet,
She insisted that all the family try it,
And all one week end we gobbled like pigs
On rutabagas and salted figs.

She clogged the pipes and she blew the fuses,
She broke the rocker that Grandma uses,
She left stuff to be posted or expressed,
Hecate Hopper, the Polterguest.

If I pushed Miss Hopper under the train
I'd probably have to do it again,
For the time that I pushed her off the boat
I regretfully found Miss Hopper could float.

A BEGINNER'S GUIDE TO THE OCEAN

Let us now consider the ocean.
It is always in motion.
It is generally understood to be the source of much of our
    rain,

And ten thousand fleets are said to have swept over it in
    vain.

When the poet requested it to break break break on its
    cold gray rocks it obligingly broke broke broke.

Which as the poet was Alfred Lord Tennyson didn't sur-
    prise him at all but if it had been me I would probably
    have had a stroke.

Some people call it the Atlantic and some the Pacific or the
    Antarctic or the Indian or the Mediterranean Sea,

But I always say what difference does it make, some old
    geographer mumbling a few words of it, it will always
    be just the Ocean to me.

There is an immortal dignity about something like the At-
    lantic,

Which seems to drive unimmortal undignified human
    beings frustratedly frantic.

Just give them one foot on the beach and people who were
    perfectly normal formerly, or whilom,

Why, they are subject to whoops and capers that would
    get them blackballed from an asylum;

Yet be they never so rampant and hollerant,

The ocean is tolerant,

Except a couple of times a day it gives up in disgust and
    goes off by itself and hides,

And that, my dears, accounts for the tides.

TABOO TO BOOT

One bliss for which
There is no match
Is when you itch
To up and scratch.

[108]

Yet doctors and dowagers deprecate scratching,
Society ranks it with spitting and snatching,
And medical circles consistently hold
That scratching's as wicked as feeding a cold.
What flame burns unquenched 'neath how many a stocking
On account of to scratch in a salon is shocking!

> 'Neath tile or thatch
> That man is rich
> Who has a scratch
> For every itch.

Ho, squirmers and writhers, how long will ye suffer
The medical tyrant, the social rebuffer!
On the edge of the door let our shoulderblades rub,
Let the drawing room now be as free as the tub!
Let us scratch notwithstanding M.D.'s and their vetoes,
And if they object, let us wish them mosquitoes.

> I'm greatly attached
> To Barbara Frietchie.
> I bet she scratched
> When she was itchy.

A WORD ON WIND

Cows go around saying Moo,
But the wind goes around saying Woooo.
Ghosts say Woooo to you, too,
And sometimes they say Boo to you, too,
But everybody has heard the wind and few people have
    heard a ghost,

So it is commonly supposed that the wind says Woooo the
   most.

Scientists try to tell us that wind is caused by atmospheric
   conditions at the North Pole or over distant Canadian
   ranches,

But I guess scientists don't ever get to the country because
   everybody who has ever been in the country knows
   that wind is caused by the trees waggling their
   branches.

On the ocean, where there are no trees, they refer to the
   wind as gales,

And it is probably caused by whales,

And in the Sahara, where there are no trees or whales
   either, they call the wind a simoom or something,

And it is the result of the profanation of Tutankhamen's
   tomb or something,

But anyhow wherever you are, the wind is always nigh and
   I for one hope it won't come any nigher,

Because it makes cold colder and heat hotter and rain wetter
   and dust drier,

And it can cover a lot of time in a very short space,

And it doesn't matter whether it's an East Wind and you
   are heading West or a North Wind and you are heading South, it always manages to be right in your face.

Ill winds blow nobody good and they also blow new hats
   into mud puddles and voracious clouds of mosquitoes
   into propinquity with your hide,

And they make your cigarette burn down on just one side.

Some people are very refined,

And when they recite poetry or sing songs they pronounce
   wind, wined.

Well, dear wined, every time you say Wooooo,

Why I wish you would say it to people who say wined,
    right after you have said it somewhere where some-
    body is making fertilizer or glue.

SHRINKING SONG

Woolen socks, woolen socks!
Full of color, full of clocks!
Plain and fancy, yellow, blue,
From the counter beam at you.
O golden fleece, O magic flocks!
O irresistible woolen socks!
O happy haberdasher's clerk
Amid that galaxy to work!
And now it festers, now it rankles
Not to have them round your ankles;
Now with your conscience do you spar;
They look expensive, and they are;
Now conscience whispers, You ought not to,
And human nature roars, You've got to!
Woolen socks, woolen socks!
First you buy them in a box.
You buy them several sizes large,
Fit for Hercules, or a barge.
You buy them thus because you think
These lovely woolen socks may shrink.
At home you don your socks with ease,
You find the heels contain your knees;
You realize with saddened heart
Their toes and yours are far apart.
You take them off and mutter Bosh,

You up and send them to the wash.
Too soon, too soon the socks return,
Too soon the horrid truth you learn;
Your woolen socks cannot be worn
Unless a midget child is born,
And either sockless you must go,
Or buy a sock for every toe.
Woolen socks, woolen socks!
Infuriating paradox!
Hosiery wonderful and terrible,
Heaven to wear, and yet unwearable.
The man enmeshed in such a quandary
Can only hie him to the laundry,
And while his socks are hung to dry,
Wear them once as they're shrinking by.

EVERYBODY HAS AN UNCLE

I wish I were a Tibetan monk
Living in a monastery.
I would unpack my trunk
And store it in a tronastery;
I would collect all my junk
And send it to a jonastery;
I would try to reform an unc-
le and pay his expenses at an onastery,
And if my income shrunk
I would send it to a shronastery.

EVERYBODY EATS TOO MUCH ANYHOW

You gulp your breakfast and glance at the clock,
Through eleventh hour packing you gallop amok,
You bundle your bags in the back of the car,
You enter, she enters, and there you are.
You clutch the wheel, she clutches the maps,
And longs for a couple of extra laps.
It's *au revoir* to your modest abode,
You're gipsies, away on the open road;
Into the highway you burst like a comet or
Heat waves climbing a Kansas thermometer.
The conversation is sweet as clover,
With breakfast practically hardly over.
"Darling, light me a cigarette?"
"At once and with all my heart, my pet;
And by the way, we are off the track;
We should have turned left a half-mile back."
You swing around with a cheery smile,
Thus far, a mile is only a mile.
The road is romance, so let it wind,
With breakfast an hour or so behind.
Under the tires the pebbles crunch,
And through the dust creep thoughts of lunch.
The speedometer sits on a steady fifty
And more and more does lunch seem nifty.
Your eyes to the road ahead are glued,
She glances about in search of food.
She sees a place. She would like to try it.
She says so. Well, you're already by it.
Ignoring the road, you spot an eatery;
The look of it makes her interior teetery.

She sees a beauty. You're past it again.
Her eyebrows look like ten past ten;
She's simmering now, and so are you,
And *your* brows register ten to two.
She snubs the excuse as you begin it —
That there'll be another one any minute —
She says there won't. It must be a plot;
She's absolutely correct. There's not.
You finally find one. You stop and alight.
You're both too annoyed to eat a bite.
Oh, this is the gist of my gipsy song:
Next time carry your lunch along.

WATER FOR THE GANDER

You take a man who has ever possessed an infant son or
daughter,
And he feels pretty superior about drinks of water.
His voice is full of paternal lenience
As he describes how their thirst is always adjusted to his
utmost inconvenience,
And you gather that there is no rest for the married,
If only because of the little ones who choose to be perpetu-
ally inopportunely arid.
I assume that these little ones have never seen their sire in
session
At his business or profession,
So listen closely, infant son and infant daughter,
His business or profession is what he carries on between
getting up to get a drink of water.
It requires a dozen visits to the nearest water cooler or
fount

Before he can face drawing up a report or balancing an
    account.
You may be interested to note
That the driest point in America is not Death Valley, but
    a man with lots of important work on his desk's throat.
Therefore, children, when he next complains at midnight
    about your everlasting thirst,
Simply ask him how many hours he spent that day at his
    desk and how many at the water cooler, and he may
    answer you, but I bet he has to go and get himself a
    drink of water first.

APARTMENT TO SUBLET — UNFURNISHED

The Murrays are hunting a house,
They are tired of living in flats.
They long for a personal mouse,
And a couple of personal cats.
They are hunting a house to inhabit,
An Eden, or even an Arden,
They are thinking of keeping a rabbit,
They are thinking of digging a garden.
How giddy the Murrays have grown,
To aspire to a house of their own!

Oh, hurry, hurry!
Says Mrs. Murray.
Tarry awhile, says he,
If you care for a house
As is a house,
You'd better leave it to me.

I'd like an orchard, apple or peach,
I'd like an accessible bathing beach,
And a den for unwinding detective plots,
And a lawn for practicing mashie shots,
And open fires,
And a pleasant sunroom,
A handy garage,
And perhaps a gunroom,
And an atmosphere exempt of static,
And a furnace silent and automatic.
For such a house
I would hurry, hurry —
I'm a practical man,
Says Mr. Murray.

The Murrays of 17 B,
The Murrays are going away,
From the wireless in 17 C,
And the parties in 17 A.
For the Murrays are tired of flats,
They are rapidly growing aloof,
As they dream of their personal cats,
As they dream of their personal roof.
Their friends cannot smother their merriment
When they speak of the Murrays' experiment.

Oh, hurry, hurry!
Says Mr. Murray.
Tarry awhile, says she.
When we choose a house,
Let us choose a house
As nice as a house can be.

With a dozen windows south and east,
And a dozen capacious cupboards at least,
And a laundry lilting with light and air,
And a porch for a person to dry her hair,
And plenty of sun,
And plenty of shade,
And a neat little place
For a neat little maid,
And a wall with roses clambering wild,
And a quiet room for a sleepy child.
If you happen to see it,
Hurry, hurry!
For *that's* the house,
Says Mrs. Murray.

YOU HAVE MORE FREEDOM IN A HOUSE

The Murrays are snug in their house,
They are finished forever with flats;
They longed for a personal mouse,
And room to swing dozens of cats.
They longed for a hearth and a doorway,
In Arden, or maybe in Eden,
But the Eden is rather like Norway,
And the Arden like winter in Sweden.
How baffled the Murrays have grown
Since they live in a house of their own!

Oh, hurry, hurry!
Says Mrs. Murray.
But listen, my dear, says he,

If you want the house
A temperate house,
You'd better not leave it to me.
I've learned the knack of swinging a cat,
But I can't coerce the thermostat.
The furnace has given a gruesome cough,
And something has cut the fuel off,
And the heart of the nursery radiator
Is cold as the prose of Walter Pater,
And I've telephoned for the service men
But they can't get here until after ten,
So swaddle the children,
And hurry, hurry —
I'm a practical man,
Says Mr. Murray.

The Murrays are vague about fuses,
And mechanical matters like that,
And each of them frequently muses
On the days when they lived in a flat.
Was the plumbing reluctant to plumb?
Was the climate suggestive of Canada?
Did the radio crackle and hum?
You simply called down to the janada!
The Murrays have found no replacement
For the genius who lived in the basement.

Oh, hurry, hurry!
Says Mr. Murray.
I'm doing my best, says she,
But it's hard to scrub
In a tepid tub,

So the guests must wait for me;
And tell them they'll get their cocktails later
When you've managed to fix the refrigerator.
And explain if the coffee looks like water,
That the stove is as queer as a seventh daughter,
And I will be down as soon as able
To unstick the drawers of my dressing table.

There's a car at the door, says Mrs. Murray,
The doorbell's broken, so hurry, hurry!
Oh, I don't regret
Being wed to you,
But I wish I could wed
A janitor too.

THE UNSELFISH HUSBAND

Once upon a time there was a man named Orlando Tregennis and he was in love with his wife,
And he thought he would express his love by serenading
her but his serenade wasn't very successful because
his playing interfered with his singing because all
he could play was the fife,
So then he said, I will climb the highest mountain in the
world and name it after my wife and then she will
give me a look of love, so he climbed the highest
mountain in the world and his wife was indeed
whom he named it after,
But she didn't give him a look of love, she gave him a
look of laughter,
And not only a look of laughter but a look of menace,

[119]

Because he named it after his wife by naming it Mt.
Mrs. Orlando Tregennis,
So then Mr. Tregennis said, Well, I haven't any gold,
But I will give you my most precious possession, I will
give you my cold,
And he gave her his cold and first of all she tried to
spurn it,
And then she tried to return it,
But he said No darling, now it's your very own cold,
It is yours to have and to hold,
Because if you reckon I don't give gifts for keeps you made
a mistake when you reckoned,
Because there hasn't been an Indian-giver in the Tregennis
family since my great-great-grandfather, old Hiawatha
Tregennis II.
But she wouldn't take no for an answer, but he wouldn't
say yes, and Mr. Tregennis's precious cold went
shuttling back and forth between them for the rest
of their lives,
And I hope everybody will turn out to be such self-
sacrificing husbands and wives.

SO PENSEROSO

Come, megrims, mollygrubs and collywobbles!
Come, gloom that limps, and misery that hobbles!
Come also, most exquisite melancholiage,
As dark and decadent as November foliage!
I crave to shudder in your moist embrace,
To feel your oystery fingers on my face.
This is my hour of sadness and of soulfulness,

And cursed be he who dissipates my dolefulness.
The world is wide, isn't it?
The world is roomy.
Isn't there room, isn't it,
For a man to be gloomy?
Bring me a bathysphere, kindly,
Maybe like Beebe's,
Leave me alone in it, kindly,
With my old heebie-jeebies.
I do not desire to be cheered,
I desire to retire, I am thinking of growing a beard,
A sorrowful beard, with a mournful, a dolorous hue in it,
With ashes and glue in it.
I want to be drunk with despair,
I want to caress my care,
I do not wish to be blithe,
I wish to recoil and writhe,
I will revel in cosmic woe,
And I want my woe to show.
This is the morbid moment,
This is the ebony hour.
Aroint thee, sweetness and light!
I want to be dark and sour!
Away with the bird that twitters!
All that glitters is jitters!
Roses, roses are gray,
Violets cry Boo! and frighten me.
Sugar is diabetic,
And people conspire to brighten me.
Go hence, people, go hence!
Go sit on a picket fence!
Go gargle with mineral oil,

Go out and develop a boil!
Melancholy is what I brag and boast of,
Melancholy I mean to make the most of,
You beaming optimists shall not destroy it.
But while I am it, I intend to enjoy it.
Go, people, feed on kewpies and soap,
And remember, please, that when I mope, I mope!

COMPLAINT TO FOUR ANGELS

Every night at sleepy-time
Into bed I gladly climb.
Every night anew I hope
That with the covers I can cope.

Adjust the blanket fore and aft,
Swallow next a soothing draught;
Then a page of Scott or Cooper
May induce a healthful stupor.

Oh, the soft luxurious darkness,
Fit for Morgan, or for Harkness!
Traffic dies along the street.
The light is out. So are your feet.

Adjust the blanket aft and fore,
Sigh, and settle down once more.
Behold, a breeze! The curtains puff.
One blanket isn't quite enough.

Yawn and rise and seek your slippers,
Which, by now, are cold as kippers.

Yawn, and stretch, and prod yourself,
And fetch a blanket from the shelf.

And so to bed again, again,
Cozy under blankets twain.
Welcome warmth and sweet nirvana
Till eight o'clock or so mañana.

You sleep as deep as Keats or Bacon;
Then you dream and toss and waken.
Where is the breeze? There isn't any.
Two blankets, boy, are one too many.

O stilly night, why are you not
Consistent in your cold and hot?
O slumber's chains, unlocked so oft
With blankets being donned or doffed!

The angels who should guard my bed
I fear are slumbering instead.
O angels, please resume your hovering;
I'll sleep, and you adjust the covering.

IT'S NEVER FAIR WEATHER

I do not like the winter wind
That whistles from the North.
My upper teeth and those beneath,
They jitter back and forth.
Oh, some are hanged, and some are skinned,
And others face the winter wind.

I do not like the summer sun
That scorches the horizon.
Though some delight in Fahrenheit,
To me it's deadly pizen.
I think that life would be more fun
Without the simmering summer sun.

I do not like the signs of spring,
The fever and the chills,
The icy mud, the puny bud,
The frozen daffodils.
Let other poets gayly sing;
I do not like the signs of spring.

I do not like the foggy fall
That strips the maples bare;
The radiator's mating call,
The dank, rheumatic air.
I fear that taken all in all,
I do not like the foggy fall.

The winter sun is always kind,
And summer wind's a savior,
And I'll merrily sing of fall and spring
When they're on their good behavior.
But otherwise I see no reason
To speak in praise of any season.

A Mrs. Shepherd of Danbury, Conn.,
She tried to steal our cook,
She may have thought to stay anon.,
But now she's in a book!
Oh — Mrs. — Shepherd,
OH! Mrs. SHEPHERD!
I'll hunt you hither, I'll hunt you yon.
Did you really hope to remain anon.?
Didn't you know the chance you took
Making a pass at a poet's cook?

Oh, Mrs. S. of the Nutmeg State,
No human shame she knew,
Her carnal appetites to sate,
Our home she walked into.
Oh — Mrs. — Shepherd!
OH! Mrs. SHEPHERD!
By hook and by crook and by telephone
You attempted to rob us of our own.
You ruptured the laws of God and man
And made a pass at Matilda Ann.

Then here's a health to Matilda Ann
Whose soups are soundly peppered,
Whose commonest meats are godlike feats,
Who resisted Mrs. Shepherd.
But — Oh — Mrs. — Shepherd!
OH! Mrs. SHEPHERD!
You ruptured the laws of man and God
When in our kitchen you softly trod.

You tiptoed hither, you tiptoed yon,
You fondly hoped to remain anon.,
But householders all, the nation over,
Shall hear the name of the lawless rover
Who by telephone and by hook and crook
Attempted to alienate our cook.
Go back to your home in Danbury, Conn.,
And carry this curse to ponder on:
I hope that your soup is washy-wishy,
Your salad sandy, your butter fishy,
Your oatmeal scorched and your sirloins boiled,
Your soufflé soggy, your sherbet oiled,
Till all your neighbors in Danbury, Conn.,
As they watch the Shepherds grow feeble and wan,
Say: "She should have thought of the chance she took,
Making a pass at a poet's cook."

TIN WEDDING WHISTLE

Though you know it anyhow
Listen to me, darling, now,

Proving what I need not prove
How I know I love you, love.

Near and far, near and far,
I am happy where you are;

Likewise I have never larnt
How to be it where you aren't.

Far and wide, far and wide,
I can walk with you beside;

Furthermore, I tell you what,
I sit and sulk where you are not.

Visitors remark my frown
When you're upstairs and I am down,

Yes, and I'm afraid I pout
When I'm indoors and you are out;

But how contentedly I view
Any room containing you.

In fact I care not where you be,
Just as long as it's with me.

In all your absences I glimpse
Fire and flood and trolls and imps.

Is your train a minute slothful?
I goad the stationmaster wrothful.

When with friends to bridge you drive
I never know if you're alive,

And when you linger late in shops
I long to telephone the cops.

Yet how worth the waiting for,
To see you coming through the door.

Somehow, I can be complacent
Never but with you adjacent.

Near and far, near and far,
I am happy where you are;

Likewise, I have never larnt
How to be it where you aren't.

Then grudge me not my fond endeavor,
To hold you in my sight forever;

Let none, not even you, disparage
Such valid reason for a marriage.

THE PERFECT HUSBAND

He tells you when you've got on
   too much lipstick,
And helps you with your girdle
   when your hips stick.

FAMILY COURT

One would be in less danger
From the wiles of the stranger
If one's own kin and kith
Were more fun to be with.

SAMSON AGONISTES

I test my bath before I sit,
And I'm always moved to wonderment
That what chills the finger not a bit
Is so frigid upon the fundament.

GOOD RIDDANCE, BUT NOW WHAT?

Come children, gather round my knee;
Something is about to be.

Tonight's December thirty-first,
Something is about to burst.

The clock is crouching, dark and small,
Like a time bomb in the hall.

Hark, it's midnight, children dear.
Duck! Here comes another year!

FRAGONARD

There was an old miser named Clarence,
Who simonized both of his parents.
"The initial expense,"
He remarked, "is immense,
But I'll save it on wearance and tearance."

THE HUNTER

The hunter crouches in his blind
'Neath camouflage of every kind,
And conjures up a quacking noise
To lend allure to his decoys.
This grown-up man, with pluck and luck,
Is hoping to outwit a duck.

FUNEBRIAL REFLECTION

Among the anthropophagi
One's friends are one's sarcophagi.

THE CARAWAY SEED

The Abbé Voltaire, alias Arouet,
Never denounced the seed of the caraway;
Sufficient proof, if proof we need,
That he never bit into a caraway seed.

CELERY

Celery, raw,
Develops the jaw,
But celery, stewed,
Is more quickly chewed.

THE PARSNIP

The parsnip, children, I repeat
Is simply an anemic beet.
Some people call the parsnip edible;
Myself, I find this claim incredible.

THE CANTALOUPE

One cantaloupe is ripe and lush,
Another's green, another's mush.
I'd buy a lot more cantaloupe
If I possessed a fluoroscope.

THE ABSENTEES

I'd ride a cock horse to Banbury Cross
For giblet gravy and cranberry sauce,
Two treats which are held in reserve by the waiter
Till you've finished your turkey and mashed potater.

LATHER AS YOU GO

Beneath this slab
John Brown is stowed.
He watched the ads,
And not the road.

SONG OF THE OPEN ROAD

I think that I shall never see
A billboard lovely as a tree.
Indeed, unless the billboards fall
I'll never see a tree at all.

NO DOCTORS TODAY, THANK YOU

They tell me that euphoria is the feeling of feeling wonder-
   ful; well, today I feel euphorian,
Today I have the agility of a Greek god and the appetite
   of a Victorian.
Yes, today I may even go forth without my galoshes;
Today I am a swashbuckler, would anybody like me to
   buckle any swashes?
This is my euphorian day,
I will ring welkins and before anybody answers I will run
   away.
I will tame me a caribou
And bedeck it with marabou.
I will pen me my memoirs.
Ah youth, youth! What euphorian days them was!
I wasn't much of a hand for the boudoirs,
I was generally to be found where the food was.
Does anybody want any flotsam?
I've gotsam.
Does anybody want any jetsam?
I can getsam.
I can play "Chopsticks" on the Wurlitzer,
I can speak Portuguese like a Berlitzer.
I can don or doff my shoes without tying or untying the
   laces because I am wearing moccasins,
And I practically know the difference between serums and
   antitoccasins.
Kind people, don't think me purse-proud, don't set me
   down as vainglorious,
I'm just a little euphorious.

TWO DOGS HAVE I

For years we've had a little dog,
Last year we acquired a big dog;
He wasn't big when we got him,
He was littler than the dog we had.
We thought our little dog would love him,
Would help him to become a trig dog,
But the new little dog got bigger,
And the old little dog got mad.

Now the big dog loves the little dog,
But the little dog hates the big dog,
The little dog is eleven years old,
And the big dog only one;
The little dog calls him *Schweinhund*,
The little dog calls him *Pig-dog*,
She grumbles broken curses
As she dreams in the August sun.

The big dog's teeth are terrible,
But he wouldn't bite the little dog;
The little dog would grind his spine,
But the little dog has no teeth;
The big dog is acrobatic,
The little dog is a brittle dog;
She leaps to grip his jugular,
And passes underneath.

The big dog clings to the little dog
Like glue and cement and mortar;
The little dog is his own true love;

But the big dog is to her
Like a scarlet rag to a Longhorn,
Or a suitcase to a porter;
The day he sat on the hornet
I distinctly heard her purr.

Well, how can you blame the little dog,
Who was once the household darling?
He romps like a young Adonis,
She droops like an old mustache;
No wonder she steals his corner,
No wonder she comes out snarling,
No wonder she calls him *Cochon*
And even *Espèce de vache.*

Yet once I wanted a sandwich,
Either caviar or cucumber,
When the sun had not yet risen
And the moon had not yet sank;
As I tiptoed through the hallways
The big dog lay in slumber,
And the little dog slept by the big dog,
And her head was on his flank.

THE VOICE OF EXPERIENCE

A husband at a lecture
Twitches his architecture.

He undergoes the lecturing
Like unanesthetized vivisecturing.

He's a glassy-eyed conjecturer
Of the ancestry of the lecturer.

Husbands hide in storerooms
To escape Town Halls and Forums.

They improvise *In Memoriams*
For speakers in auditoriums.

They regard as nauseous nostrums
Opinions delivered from rostrums.

They feel about orators' rhetorics
Like Cæsar about Vercingetorix.

They flinch as the fog of boredom
Creeps verbosely toredom.

Their collars grow more and more cumbersome,
And at last they essay to slumber some.

But this respite their spouses grudge them,
And if they nod, they nudge them.

There is none so irate and awkward
As a husband being Chautauquard.

GEDDONDILLO

The sharrot scudders nights in the quastron now,
The dorlim slinks undeceded in the grost,
Appetency lights the corb of the guzzard now,
The ancient beveldric is otley lost.

Treduty flees like a darbit along the drace now,
Collody lollops belutedly over the slawn.
The bloodbound bitterlitch bays the ostrous moon now,
For yesterday's bayable majicity is flunkly gone.

Make way, make way, the preluge is scarly nonce now,
Make way, I say, the gronderous Demiburge comes,
His blidless veins shall ye joicily rejugulate now,
And gollify him from 'twixt his protecherous gums.

A PLEA FOR A LEAGUE OF SLEEP

Some people lead a feverish life,
For they with restlessness are rife.
They revel in labors energetic,
Their fare is healthful and ascetic,
Their minds are keen, their hands are earthy,
Each day they work on something worthy.
Something accomplished, something done,
Comprises their idea of fun.

My life with joy is sometimes fraught,
But mostly when I'm doing naught.
Yea, I could spend my whole career

A pillow underneath my ear.
How wise was he who wittily said
That there is nothing like a bed.
A mattress is what I like to creep on;
The left side is the one I sleep on.

Heroes who moil and toil and fight
Exist on eight hours' sleep a night.
I call this but a miserly budget,
Yet I assure you that they grudge it.
I've heard them groan, times without number,
At wasting a third of their lives in slumber.
All right, you Spartans who build and delve,
You waste eight hours, and I'll waste twelve.

No honester man is to be found
Than he who sleeps the clock around.
Of malice and ambition free,
The more he sleeps, the sleepier he.
No plots and schemes infest his head,
But dreams of getting back to bed.
His spirit bears no worldly taint;
Scratch a sluggard, and find a saint.

Stalin and Hitler while they sleep
Are harmless as a baby sheep;
Tyrants who cause the earth to quake
Are only dangerous when awake.
This world would be a happier place,
And happier the human race,
And all our pilots be less Pontius,
If people spent more time unconscious.

OUT IS OUT

Come in, dear guests, we've got a treat for you,
We've prepared a different place to eat for you!
Guess where we're going to have our dinner!
Everyone guess! Who'll be the winner?
The dining room? Heavens! It's hereby stated
That dining rooms are dreadfully dated.
What in the world could be more plebeian
Than to eat in a place in which you can see in!
The living room? No, you're off the path;
No, not the bedroom; no, not the bath;
And not the cellar; and not the attic;
The kitchen? No, that's too democratic.
Do you all give up? Well, listen and hark:
We're going to dine outdoors, in the dark!
No lights, because there aren't any plugs,
And anyhow, lights attract the bugs,
And anyhow, in the dark we've found
There are bugs enough to go around.
Oh, it's drizzling a little; I think perhaps
The girls had better keep on their wraps;
Just strike a match and enjoy the way
The raindrops splash in the consommé.
You probably won't get botts or pellagra
From whatever lit on your pâté de foie gras.
Now, you're not expected to eat with skill,
And everybody's supposed to spill;
If your half-broiled chicken leaps about,
That's half the excitement of eating out;
If you dust it with sugar instead of salt,
It's everyone's fun and nobody's fault;

And if anything flies in your mouth, perchance,
Why, that is mystery, that's romance!
Such a frolic and such a lark
It is to eat outdoors in the dark!
The dandiest fun since I don't know when;
Would you eat in a stuffy old room again?
Oh yes you would, you politest of liars,
And I'll see you tomorrow at the cleaner's and dyer's.

EPSTEIN, SPARE THAT YULE LOG!

When I was but a boy,
'Twas my once-a-yearly joy
To arise of a Yuletide morning,
And eagerly behold
The crimson and the gold
Of the messages the mantelpiece adorning.
There were angels, there were squires,
There were steeples, there were spires,
There were villagers, and mistletoe and holly,
There were cosy English inns
With the snow around their chins,
And I innocently thought them rather jolly.
I blush for me, but by your leave,
I'm afraid that I am still naïve.

Oh, give me an old-fashioned Christmas card,
With mistletoe galore, and holly by the yard,
With galumptious greens and gorgeous scarlets,
With crackling logs and apple-cheeked varlets,
With horses prancing down a frosty road,
And a stagecoach laden with a festive load,

[139]

And the light from the wayside windows streaming,
And a white moon rising and one star gleaming.

Departed is the time
Of Christmases sublime;
My soprano is now a mezzo-basso;
And the mantelpiece contains
The angular remains
Of a later representative Picasso.
There are circles, there are dots,
There are corners, there are spots,
There are modernistic snapshots of the city;
Or, when the artist lags,
They are livened up with gags.
You must choose between the arty and the witty.
I blush for me, but I must say
I wish you'd take them all away.

Oh, give me an old-fashioned Christmas card,
With hostlers hostling in an old inn yard,
With church bells chiming their silver notes,
And jolly red squires in their jolly red coats,
And a good fat goose by the fire that dangles,
And a few more angels and a few less angles.
Turn backward, Time, to please this bard,
And give me an old-fashioned Christmas card.

THE TROUBLE WITH WOMEN IS MEN

A husband is a man who two minutes after his head
   touches the pillow is snoring like an overloaded
   omnibus,

Particularly on those occasions when between the humidity and the mosquitoes your own bed is no longer a bed, but an insomnibus,

And if you turn on the light for a little reading he is sensitive to the faintest gleam,

But if by any chance you are asleep and he wakeful, he is not slow to rouse you with the complaint that he can't close his eyes, what about slipping downstairs and freezing him a cooling dish of pistachio ice cream.

His touch with a bottle opener is sure,

But he cannot help you get a tight dress over your head without catching three hooks and a button in your coiffure.

Nor can he so much as wash his ears without leaving an inch of water on the bathroom linoleum,

But if you mention it you evoke not a promise to splash no more but a mood of deep melancholium.

Indeed, each time he transgresses your chance of correcting his faults grows lesser,

Because he produces either a maddeningly logical explanation or a look of martyrdom which leaves you instead of him feeling the remorse of the transgressor.

Such are husbandly foibles, but there are moments when a foible ceases to be a foible.

Next time you ask for a glass of water and when he brings it you have a needle almost threaded and instead of setting it down he stands there holding it out to you, just kick him fairly hard in the stomach; you will find it thoroughly enjoible.

FOR A GOOD DOG

My little dog ten years ago
Was arrogant and spry,
Her backbone was a bended bow
For arrows in her eye.
Her step was proud, her bark was loud,
Her nose was in the sky,
But she was ten years younger then,
And so, by God, was I.

Small birds on stilts along the beach
Rose up with piping cry,
And as they flashed beyond her reach
I thought to see her fly.
If natural law refused her wings,
That law she would defy,
For she could hear unheard-of things,
And so, at times, could I.

Ten years ago she split the air
To seize what she could spy;
Tonight she bumps against a chair,
Betrayed by milky eye.
She seems to pant, Time up, time up!
My little dog must die,
And lie in dust with Hector's pup;
So, presently, must I.

PROCRASTINATION IS ALL OF THE TIME

Torpor and sloth, torpor and sloth,
These are the cooks that unseason the broth.
Slothor and torp, slothor and torp
The directest of bee-line ambitions can warp.
He who is slothic, he who is torporal,
Will not be promoted to sergeant or corporal.
No torporer drowsy, no comatose slother
Will make a good banker, not even an author.
Torpor I deprecate, sloth I deplore,
Torpor is tedious, sloth is a bore.
Sloth is a bore, and torpor is tedious,
Fifty parts comatose, fifty tragedious.
How drear, on a planet redundant with woes,
That sloth is not slumber, nor torpor repose.
That the innocent joy of not getting things done
Simmers sulkily down to plain not having fun.
You smile in the morn like a bride in her bridalness
At the thought of a day of nothing but idleness.
By midday you're slipping, by evening a lunatic,
A perusing-the-newspapers-all-afternoonatic,
Worn to a wraith from the half-hourly jaunt
After glasses of water you didn't want,
And at last when onto your pallet you creep,
You discover yourself too tired to sleep.
O torpor and sloth, torpor and sloth,
These are the cooks that unseason the broth.
Torpor is harrowing, sloth it is irksome —
Everyone ready? Let's go out and worksome.

SONG FOR A TEMPERATURE OF A
HUNDRED AND ONE

Of all God's creatures give me man
For impractical uniqueness,
He's hardly tenth when it comes to strength,
But he leads the field in weakness.
Distemper suits the ailing dog,
The chicken's content with pip,
But the human race, which sets the pace,
Takes nothing less than grippe.

THEN, hey for the grippe, for the goodly la grippe!
In dogs it's distemper, in chickens it's pip;
But the lords of creation insist at the least
On the germ that distinguishes man from the beast.

The mule with mange is satisfied,
Or hookworm in the South;
And the lowly kine will stand in line
To get their hoof-and-mouth;
Bubonic cheers the humble rat
As he leaves the sinking ship;
When the horse gets botts he thinks it's lots,
But people hold out for grippe.
THEN, hey for the grippe, for the goodly la grippe,
For the frog in the throat and the chap on the lip;
For the ice on the feet and the fire on the brow,
And the bronchial tubes that moo like a cow.
And hey for the ache in the back of the legs,
And the diet of consommé, water and eggs,
For the mustard that sits on your chest like a cactus,

For the doctor you're kindly providing with practus;
And hey for the pants of which you're so fond,
And the first happy day they're allowed to be donned;
For the first day at work, all bundled in wraps,
And last but not least, for the splendid relapse.
So let man meet his Maker, a smile on his lip,
Singing hey, double hey, for the goodly la grippe.

A WORD ABOUT WINTER

Now the frost is on the pane,
Rugs upon the floor again,
Now the screens are in the cellar,
Now the student cons the speller,
Lengthy summer noon is gone,
Twilight treads the heels of dawn,
Round-eyed sun is now a squinter,
Tiptoe breeze a panting sprinter,
Every cloud a blizzard hinter,
Squirrel on the snow a printer,
Rainspout sprouteth icy splinter,
Willy-nilly, this is winter.

Summer-swollen doorjambs settle,
Ponds and puddles turn to metal,
Skater whoops in frisky fettle,
Golf club stingeth like a nettle,
Radiator sings like kettle,
Hearth is popocatepetl.

Runneth nose and chappeth lip,
Draft evadeth weather strip,

Doctor wrestleth with grippe
In never-ending rivalship.
Rosebush droops in garden shoddy,
Blood is cold and thin in body,
Weary postman dreams of toddy,
Head before the hearth grows noddy.
On the hearth the embers gleam,
Glowing like a maiden's dream,
Now the apple and the oak
Paint the sky with chimney smoke,
Husband now, without disgrace,
Dumps ash trays in the fireplace.

THE MIDDLE

When I remember bygone days
I think how evening follows morn;
So many I loved were not yet dead,
So many I love were not yet born.